Special Purchase
100
B

KAHLIL GIBRAN:
THE NATURE OF LOVE

KAHLIL GIBRAN:
THE NATURE OF LOVE

by

ANDREW DIB SHERFAN

PHILOSOPHICAL LIBRARY
New York

Distributed to the Trade by
BOOK SALES, INC.
110 Enterprise Avenue
Secaucus N.J. 07094

Manufactured in the United States of America

DEDICATION

This work is dedicated to the First Family of the Philippines as representatives of the fine Filipino people whose hospitality I have enjoyed and admired for the years that I have lived in their beloved country.

It is also dedicated to the hundreds of Filipino youths, whom I have had the privilege of teaching at La Salle Green Hills, and who impressed me so much by their gentleness and superior qualities. Among such youths was Ferdinand Marcos, Jr., the son of the First Family.

FOREWORD

It has been my privilege to suggest that Brother Andrew Sherfan, F.S.C. write a study on the works of his compatriot, the poet Kahlil Gibran.

My reasons for making the suggestion were threefold.

First, while Kahlil Gibran, whom I consider to be among the great poets in more recent times, is immensely popular in his native Lebanon and has quite a following in the United States, he is practically unknown, except among the literati, in other parts of the world. A study of his poetry, therefore, would introduce him to a wider reading public in this part of the world.

Second, Brother Andrew Sherfan is himself a Lebanese: he is thus in a very good position to grasp the many nuances, subtleties and insights so necessary in a study of Gibran's poetry.

Third, Gibran has touched on the human condition, and his pronouncements, in cadences reminiscent of the majesty of Biblical lines, are as valid and as relevant today as when he first wrote them.

Happily, Brother Andrew Sherfan accepted the suggestion. Using Arabic, English and French sources, not to say all the works of Gibran available to him, and drawing from his intimate knowledge of the country and the various influences of the time that produced Kahlil Gibran, Brother Andrew has brought to a successful conclusion a study which, to my mind, is as perceptive as it is deep.

While Brother Sherfan focuses his attention only on one aspect of Gibran's works, analysing as he does the various

7

phases of love as may be seen in Gibran's great poems, that is to say, the love between man and woman, parent and child, man and God, man and society, and man and state, it is Kahlil Gibran who is made to speak for himself most of the time: so liberal are the citations from Gibran's works to illustrate major themes. Thus, after a perusal of Brother Andrew's study, the reader has also savoured the breadth and depth and mystic feeling of Gibran's poems so that it seems almost inescapable that he will want to read the works themselves.

Ultimately, it is the heart and mind and soul of Gibran that are laid bare, and one catches there glimpses of deep insights into the human condition that only a Kahlil Gibran can articulate in the sweeping majesty of his lines.

Indeed, Kahlil Gibran speaks to the modern man about problems that cry out for solution. To an age beset by problems of senseless wars and needless killings, of the ever-widening gap between rich and poor, of races exploiting others, and of the crisis of faith and belief, Kahlil Gibran speaks in a clear, unmistakable voice, and always with affection, compassion and sympathy.

Brother Andrew Sherfan has provided us with a handy guide by which we may listen to that voice. It is my hope that Brother Sherfan's work will find ready acceptance by the audience that it seeks to address itself.

MARCELINO A. FORONDA, Ph.D.
Associate Professor of History
and Literature

De La Salle College
Manila, Philippines
15 May 1970
Feast of St. John Baptist de la Salle

CONTENTS

INTRODUCTION

No one can seriously claim that he does not need to love or be loved by others. Love is at the center of life whether we like to admit it or not. Any person whose nature is normal is attracted by tenderness, a show of love, affection and sympathy. A normal male and a normal female are mutually attracted. Invading as it does the details of daily life, love is of great interest to each one of us regardless of our social status. Each one is interested in knowing what are the attitudes of other people towards this major influence in life. The child, the teenager, the lover, the wife, the husband, the elderly man, the weak, the oppressed and even the criminal, feel the need of love, and through it they certainly note a tremendous change in their lives.

The strength and dynamism of love are known to all people. History is full of instances where catastrophes and wars were brought about by uncontrolled love. The famous siege and destruction of Troy was triggered by a romantic motive — the rescue of Helen, reportedly the most beautiful woman of antiquity.[1]

Cleopatra's beauty has become proverbial after it prompted the armies of Julius Caesar to fight in the Alexandrian War and thus helped the charming queen regain her rights. The same seductive beauty also fascinated Mark Antony who fought for her and took her as his mistress. This *folie à deux* brought about Antony's suicide when he mistakenly heard that his sweetheart had died.[2]

1. *Encyclopedia Americana,* Vol. 27, p. 83.
2. *Encyclopedia Britannica,* Vol. 5, p. 801.

We are all familiar with the beheading of Saint John the Baptist that is reported by Saint Matthew. Herodias' daughter danced at a banquet and charmed Herod who at her request ordered the decapitation of Christ's forerunner who was then in jail for reproaching Herodias' romance with Philip, the King's brother.[1]

Just as love has inspired these atrocities in the history of mankind, love has also been the driving force for thousands of people to leave country and comfort in order to serve the poor, the ignorant, and the hungry. Father Damien dedicated his life to the service of the lepers on the Molokai Islands; Albert Schweitzer lived among the sick of Africa; and even today, Mr. Raoul Follereau is dedicating his life to build hospitals for the world's ten million lepers.

Love is indeed, as Gibran says, a burning fire, consuming and destroying. Love is a double-edged weapon, desired yet feared by all. Novels are full of love-stories showing man either as the victim, or the hero of his love. Love is a great and important factor in life, yet for many the source of unsolved problems. The more people write about it, the more puzzling and mysterious it becomes.

The purpose of this book is to study love under its various aspects according to the famous Lebanese writer, mystic and philosopher, Gibran Kahlil Gibran. Since he appears to be the idol of millions throughout the world, mainly in the United States, it seems opportune to study his writings which are full of Oriental mysticism; symbolism and metaphors. It is only after having read his works that the author of this paper found himself struck by his deep sense of love expressed in typical Oriental imagery. This is doubtless the reason why Gibran has a special appeal to those anxious souls who do not find an exit out of the prison that love has created for them. They seem to be simultaneously choked by honey and bitterness. In fact, Gibran's doctrine has this double factor which is quite alluring for those who face a

1. *Saint Matthew*, XIV, 1-12.

love-crisis. This does not mean that everything Gibran advocates is orthodox or reasonable. In many places, he seems to have a special gift of expressing the depth as well as the strength of love with its sweetness and its bitterness.

PREFACE

KAHLIL GIBRAN'S PHILOSOPHY OF LOVE
NO MAN IS AN ISLAND

> ". . . each man is an island unto himself, and the bridges
> that lead to other people have been destroyed by conflicts
> of race, sex and self interest. Torment and anguish inflict
> (men's) hearts, & love which can be their only solace has
> been quarantined by the individual ego and the social
> code. Bred on self doubt and their uncertain knowledge
> of others, : . . people struggle against the confusion of
> their own emotional and intellectual entanglements, seek-
> ing momentary pleasures, and finding continual disil-
> lusionment."
>
> *Robert Donald Spector*

The quotation from Robert Spector is a grim picture of
the world, but unfortunately it is a rather accurate one. We
live in a world that destroys the bridges between men.
Threatened by others, by the problems of law and order,
the mistrust of government officials, the threat of revolution,
and afraid to walk the streets at night, we tear the bridges
down and retreat behind our walls and the security of a
locked gate. We read of the problems of others — the thousands who do not have enough to eat, who cannot educate
their children or plan for a better tomorrow. We take love,
which can be the only solution, and quarantine it in a little
room.

We share our love only with our children, only with our
friends, and refuse to share it with those million others who
need it so much. The tragedy of our lives is the wall we
build around our house and the glass we put on top of the
wall and the lock we put on our front gate, because they
are a symbol of the wall we have put around our hearts.
"I am a rock," the folk song says, "I am an island. I've built
a wall . . . that none may penetrate. I am a rock, I am an
island. If I had never loved, I never would have cried."

Yet of all the commodities in our world, love is the only

one we lose when we keep it. We know that every day men are dying of hunger, that men live in slums, that many cannot earn a decent day's salary, that many are illiterate, that they have no hope of a better life for their children.

When we know this and do nothing about it, we only condemn ourselves to death. When love is quarantined, it withers away and dies, and after a while we find that there isn't any love for the children, there isn't any love for ourselves.

Yet we persist in locking love up in a little room because of the individual ego and the social code — because of our own selfishness and because everybody else does it. If only we had the courage to embark upon what Chardin calls the great adventure of universal love and to ignore the raised eyebrows of our friends and neighbors! How often we fail because we are not sure of ourselves or because we really do not know what goes on in the hearts of others. If we had the courage to reach out first, how many there are who would join us! But "I have my books," the folk song goes on, "and my poetry to protect me, and shielded in my armor, hiding in my room, I touch no one and no one touches me. I am a rock, I am an island, and a rock feels no pain and an island never cries."

There is a strange paradox in all of this. Although many others need us, and some of them need us very badly, we also need them, and some of us need them very badly. Those in need help us to grow, to be more of a person ourselves. It is a constantly recurring miracle of human existence that a man grows when someone else needs him, and he responds with all the power at his command.

There is a beautiful passage in Paul Claudel that expresses this deeply human realization: "Not one of our fellowmen, even if he wished, could fail us, and in the most unfeeling miser, in the innermost being of the prostitute and the most foul drunkard there is an immortal soul intent on keeping itself alive, and which, shut out from the light of day, worships in the night. I hear them speaking when we speak

16

and weeping when I kneel to pray. I accept all this! I reach out to them all, I comprehend them all. There is not one that I do not need or that I can do without." I am my brother's keeper. I dare not turn my back on his needs without turning my back on my own needs as a person. I cannot deny him love, without losing it myself.

St. James says: "If one of the brothers or one of the sisters is in need of clothes, and has not enough food to live on, and one of you says to them: "I wish you well; keep yourself warm and eat plenty," without giving them these bare necessities of life, then what good is that?" (James 2:15-16). We cannot say to ourselves that it is their fault if they are in need. They ought to work harder and do something about it themselves. Nor can we say that the problems are too big for us to solve alone. There is too much poverty in the world, too much dishonesty, too much hatred and too much violence. What can I possibly do about it with the little that I have at my disposal?

Christ became man 2000 years ago to build bridges — between heaven and earth, and between men. In a rather startling statement He identified himself with all those suffering, and all those in the Last Judgment, what will Christ say to you? "There was hunger in your country and you gave them to eat; there was injustice and dishonesty and you did your best to remove it; there were people in need and you reached out to them." Or will He say: "You did not feed the hungry; you did not give drink to the thirsty; there was crime and injustice and you were afraid and you locked yourself away from it; you never talked with a person who was poor or in need." As we live our lives each day there is a gift that all of us can give, no matter how poor in money or talent: Hold out your hand, and let your heart be in it. Brother Andrew's perceptive discussion of Gibran's philosophy of love will make it immensely easier for us all to give that gift of self.

JOSEPH A. GALDON, S.J.
Ateneo de Manila University

CHAPTER I

BACKGROUND

The Near East. The Near East is held by historians
as the birthplace of our civilization; then it spread over the
world with its various religions, cultures and philosophies.[1]
Since Gibran was born and educated in Lebanon, the crown
of the Near East and its replica in miniature, our work would
be incomplete if we did not say a word of this tremendous
influence on our author.

Before Christ, the Near Easterners were the first people
to receive a revelation from God. With the coming of Christ,
they were the first to follow him and also to betray him. St.
Paul and other apostles faithfully preached the message of
Christ to the then known world. After the rise of the Prophet
of Islam who was shocked by pagan living, idolatry and de-
cadence,[2] his followers, armed with their faith and the
sword, crossed the borders of their country,[3] spread their
belief to millions of non-believers and then confronted the
West with their strength. Christianity, which trembled and
felt threatened for the first time since its miraculous spread,
fought fire with fire, and opposed the Moslem faith with their
own Christian faith. Lepanto stands as the living record in
the hearts of Christians who defeated what they thought to
be the Anti-Christ.

With the spread of Islam, the culture of the Arab world
followed. And while the universities of Salamanca, Seville,
Baghdad and Alexandria were busy computing the number

of stars and wrestling with calculus and other sophisticated formulae of mathematics and physics. Westerners were still living in the dark ages.[4] It was during that prosperity and glory that the Arabs left to the world the legacy of Alghazal, Averroes, Avicenna and Avempace.[5]

History repeats itself. When the Arab Empire collapsed, the Arabs, as though tired of past glories, slept under the yoke of the Turkish Empire. For nearly four hundred years[6] they lived under subjugation and sterility. Then the British came, encouraged them to shake off the yoke of the Ottoman Empire[7] and challenged them to match the rest of the world in civilization and progress. France and Britain, acting for their own convenience, divided the whole area into small countries.[8] Soon the twentieth century came and with it progress. But the Arabs were still feeling their way after a long sleep. They are still in search of union; up till now, they have succeeded in agreeing on only one point, that is, to disagree.

Lebanon. Amidst the turmoil of conquests, downfalls and rivalries, Lebanon[9] was the only area untouched by any foreign power. United in their Roman Catholic faith under the leadership of Saint Maron,[10] the Lebanese fought the early heresies that threatened the Christian world. And thus have they always been in sympathy with the West rather than with the East.

Since it is the cradle of the three great monotheistic religions,[11] Lebanon has a tradition of harmony among people of many beliefs. Its motto is: "Religion for God, and the country for all". But near the end of the Ottoman Empire, Lebanon suffered hardships and near economic collapse, so that thousands of its sons emigrated to seek a better life.[12] These "Pilgrim Fathers" have brought Lebanon world fame. First among these was Gibran who, thanks to his writings done in the United States and which leaked into the active intelligentsia of the Arab World, sparked the Arab's fight for emancipation in collaboration with other eminent Lebanese emigrants. These valiant men left the legacy of world figures like Doctor Michael Debakey, considered the best heart surgeon in the United States; Doctor Peter Medawar, head of the British Medical Association and Nobel Prize winner; Alfred Kazin, a world known literary critic; Danny Thomas, the famous comedian of the United States television and movies; Charles Habib, a prominent member of the team negotiating peace in the Paris Peace Talks; and thousands of others, from the forty-seven men of Lebanese extraction in the Congress of Brazil to the last Lebanese gold traders in the remote regions of the Transvaal.

It is to this group of valiant emigrants that Gibran belongs. Lebanon always considers its sons as being Lebanese even when they have taken other citizenships.[13] Papers do not change the real identity of the wandering sons of the Holy Cedars.

THE ARABIC LANGUAGE — A "SWEET EXERCISE"

Gibran wrote almost half of his works in his native Arabic. Even to the very end of his life he continued this "sweet exercise". Many times during the making of the book *Jesus, The Son of Man* the poet broke into a flood of Arabic because he could not find an English word that conveyed the exact meaning of what he wanted to express, there being, as he said, "fifty words in Arabic to give expression to the many aspects of love," while in English there is but one.[14] Very often he complained of his inadequacy to express all his thoughts in English, despite the fact that the *Manchester Guardian* places him among six contemporary writers in English, including Joseph Conrad.

Very often Gibran would read aloud from Arabic, for the sheer pleasure of the sound. He enjoyed reading his Bible in Arabic, and he criticized the inadequacy of the translation of some verses, for he was very familiar with every nuance of the Aramaic that Jesus spoke.[15]

It is true that Arabic is rich in words and can so express many nuances of a word which could have hundreds and even thousands of synonyms. Klineberg, commenting on the Arab's concern with camel, says there are about six thousand names connected in some way with "camel", including words derived from the camel and attributes associated with it.[16]

Arabic is the most important Semitic language today. Barbara Young in *This Man from Lebanon* says that three hundred million people speak Arabic. However, the writer cannot agree as he believes that Arabic is spoken only by approximately eight million people.[17] Probably Miss Young is confusing those who speak Arabic with those who write their language in Arabic script. These include peoples of Pakistan, Persia, Indonesia, Malaysia, India, and some other countries of Moslem faith.

Arabic has twenty-eight letters which are an adaptation from the Aramaic, which in turn comes from the Phoenician. All the letters are consonantal, vowels being signs inserted above or below the letters. The majority of words have only three consonants. For instance, in the word kataba which means "to write", all the vowels are not written. What is written are the three consonants *ktb* only. With other variations we get:

katib	:	a writer	Plural:	*kuttab,* writers	
Kitab	:	a book	plural:	*kutub,* books	
kitabi	:	my book	plural:	*kutubi,* my books	
*kitabu*na :		our book	plural:	*kitabukunna,* your book (she)	
kitabuki :		thy book (she)	plural:	*kitabu*hum, their book	
*kitabu*hu :		his book			
*kitabu*ka :		thy book	plural:	*kutubu*ka, thy books	

There are two kinds of Arabic: *al lughat al fus'ha* the language of eloquence, and *al lughat al amiyya* the popular language. One can speak the popular language and still be

22

unable to speak or write or read the *al fus'ha*. But actually thanks to news media, the Arab world is trying to find a mid-way solution to this difficulty by creating a middle language *al lughat al wusta* which is used in the daily newspapers and popular radio broadcasts.

Arabic has not changed rapidly as has English. This is due partly to the fact that the Koran — the Holy Book of the Moslems — was written in Arabic and the faithful are unwilling to admit any change in it. Prayers throughout the Moslem world from Russia to Africa, and from Indonesia to the Philippines are said in Arabic which is considered the language that God chose to "reveal the Book".

For many centuries Europe was eager to learn Arabic in order to study science that was at its height in the universities of Salamanca, Alexandria and Baghdad. *The Encyclopedia Britannica* even says that it was a suitable medium for expressing Greek thought for many centuries.[18]

It was in this poetic language, full of symbolism and metaphors in which Gibran thought, meditated and wrote many of his world-famous books.

GIBRAN'S LIFE

Bsharreh, the birthplace of K. Gibran, is situated on the top of one of the highest mountains of Lebanon, near the Holy Cedars which grew at an altitude of four thousand meters. The father of Gibran was Kahlil ben Gibran, ben Saad, ben Youssef, ben Gibran. He had blonde hair and blue eyes. His work was to count the sheep of a sheep owner of the region.[19]

The mother was the daughter of the priest Estephane Abdel Kader, a slender brunette and very clever. She was the widow of Hanna Abdel Salam with whom she had emigrated to Brazil. After his death she returned to her parents with her son. Gibran fell in love with her and married her.[20]

Gibran's grandfather, after whom our author was named, was a very proud man. It is said that once a certain bishop, a friend of the local authorities, sent him an insulting letter. He addressed the messenger in a burst of anger: "Tell him that Syria is the greatest province in all the Turkish Empire; that Lebanon is the crown of Syria. Bsharri is the brightest jewel in that crown. Gibran is the most distinguished family name in Bsharri, and I am the illustrious head of that goddam family".[21]

Gibran Khalil Gibran* was born on January 6, 1883, at Bsharreh, Lebanon. He went to the village school like other boys of his age and learned Arabic, Syriac, the catechism and the psalms of David. These he knew by heart.[22] He did not like the difficult rules of the Arabic language and he called them ridiculous.[23]

His mother used to read to him tales of Arab heroes such as Harun El Rashid and the Hunting Songs of Abu N'was.[24] He liked storms and tempests. One day he was scolded by his mother for having gone under the heavy rain, just to be under the stormy weather.[25] Very often he used to seclude himself in a room where he would fall in admiration at Leonardo da Vinci's paintings for hours.[26]

In 1896, the economic situation in Lebanon deteriorated and the Gibrans, like thousands of other Lebanese, headed for the New World in search of a living. Gibran went to Boston with his mother, his half-brother Peter and his two younger sisters. There in Hudson Street, near Boston's Chinatown, the ambitious Peter secured employment while the mother and the sisters worked with their needles.[27] The young Khalil was sent to a public school with young Americans.[28]

During his adolescent life he fell into the traps of a wicked woman[29] who brought his moral life to a very low ebb. His mother felt this and insisted on sending him back to Lebanon under the excuse of learning Arabic and French at a Beirut School.[30] He returned to Lebanon in 1896 where he learned medicine, international law, the history of religion and music. He matriculated at the College de la Sagesse at Beirut. He also edited a school magazine called *Al Haqiqat*, 'The Truth'.[31] At sixteen he first appeared in print. He also made drawings of several pre-Islamic poets such as Al Farid, Abu N'was, and Al Mutanabbi.*

After his studies, in 1901, he studied painting for three years. He wrote *Spirits Rebellious* which was burnt in the market place of Beirut soon after publication. For the writing of this book Gibran was formally exiled from his country and excommunicated from the Maronite Catholic Church, as the book was pronounced "dangerous, revolutionary and poisonous to youth".[32]

In 1903 he was called back to the United States by the death of his half-brother and his youngest sister, and by the fatal illness of his mother.[33] He continued to paint and write in Arabic. By chance he met and became the friend of Miss Mary Haskel who also became his benefactress. In 1908 he went again to Paris to study at the *Académie Julien* and at the *Beaux Arts*.[34]

While in Paris, he met and made portraits of numerous distinguished persons, among them Auguste Rodin, Henri de Rochefort, Debussy, Maurice Maeterlinck, the younger Garibaldi and Edmond Rostand.[35]

In 1910 he returned to Boston and later took up residence in New York City at 51 West Tenth Street, the first studio building ever to be built in the United States for the exclusive use of painters and sculptors.[36] He lived there until his last illness.

Gibran died at Saint Vincent's Hospital, New York City on April 10, 1931, at the age of 48.[37] After much honor given to his remains in the United States, the body was taken to Lebanon draped with the Stars and Stripes and the Lebanese flag on the ship Providence.[38]

He was received in Beirut as the greatest Lebanese who ever lived and was buried in the convent of Saint Sarkees in his home village of Bsharreh.[39] To this day people visit his tomb as on a pilgrimage.[40]

THE VOICE OF THE MASTER

Gibran produced many works which were published in various places under different titles. We shall rather place his various works under those titles which are familiar to the public, although they might be published in other volumes bearing different titles.

Spirits Rebellious: (1908). This book has four stories under the form of sermons and parables. The first, *Wardeh Al Haneh*, tells the story of an unhappy woman who married a person she does not love. The second, *The Bridal Couch*, is the tale of an unhappy girl who was forced into marriage by custom and tradition rather than out of love. Frustrated, she slays her lover who refused to marry her when she ran to him during the wedding festivities, and then she slays herself and lies near his corpse. The third, *Khalil the Heretic*, awakens the people to the presence of evil men and evil things in their midst and bids them to cast away their chains and fetters and appear once more as free children of God. The fourth, *The Cry of the Graves*, is a story of the oppression of the weak at the hands of the strong; the crushing of a people's liberty by a tyrannous authority, and of the condemning of innocent men and women by judges set up in office by corrupt hands. It was this book which was burnt in the market place of Beirut.

The Broken Wings (1912). Gibran relates living facts of his life under various names. The main topic is that of his frustrated love with his village girl Hala Dhaher, whom he could not marry because she was destined to marry the bishop's nephew. The book is a Freudian compensation of his unrealized dream. It created a big turmoil in the Arab World.

A Tear and a Smile (1914). The work is of a Nietzschean inspiration in which pain and love are always together. The book is supposed to have been inspired during his meeting with Hala Dhaher, whom he saw weeping one day. At

Gibran's inquiry she simply answered, after wiping away her tears: "It's a tear and a smile".

The Madman (1918). Gibran takes a madman as his mouthpiece and lets him speak something like Nietzsche's *Thus Spake Zarathustra.* In it Gibran saw the light and found that in man, God, and the world there is an indivisible unity. He praises strength but chides cowardice and surrender. *The Madman* is the first step towards divine self-denial.

The Procession (1918). This is a dialogue between two persons. The first expresses his anger against life, evil, and oppression, and accuses people of being like machines, or slaves to the ambitious. The second, like Rousseau, praises country life where no sorrow exists, where there are no worries, no punishment, no oppression.

The Tempests (1920). In this book there is something of Valery. It is a collection of articles, stories full of explosive Nietzschean style. It is the dynamite that was sown by Nietzsche that explodes here in giving his outlook on life, world and man. He praises the strong, but also helps the weak to get stronger.

The Forerunner (1920). He tries to ridicule those who think that they are the only people who know the truth. He used the old Oriental way of satire disguised under some kind of parables used previously by famous Arab writers such as Ebenl MouQaffah, who did not enjoy freedom of speech. He also tries to show that we alone are responsible for our destiny.

The Prophet (1923). This book is considered as his masterpiece. In this work, which was translated into more than twenty languages, he used Almustafa as his mouthpiece to speak on various vital topics interesting man: love, marriage, money, giving, etc. Gibran later confided that this book is "a part of myself".

The Garden of the Prophet (1933). Published posthumously, it describes the relation between man and nature. We reel poignantly his love for the dew-drop, for the falling snow, for the stone in the path, the slumbering groves

27

and the vineyards. In it he left a simple and profound profession of faith concerning that which lies beyond the door of death.

Sand and Foam (1926). It is a link between *The Prophet* and *Jesus, The Son of Man* (1928). Man is walking on a pathway of the seashore where the tide effaces his steps and wind goes with the foam. There is no Nietzschean influence here. In it he says: "O Lord, let me be the prey of the lion, before you let the rabbit be my prey".

Jesus, The Son of Man (1928). Gibran wrote this book at the end of his life. He considers it as the crowning of his life and mission. It is not a historical work, but he portrays Jesus as having lived out life to its full with its pain and happiness. Gibran denies the divinity of Christ. He uses seventy-seven persons, each of whom speaks in his way of this "extraordinary man, Jesus". The last person is a man from Lebanon, clearly Gibran himself, who lives in the Twentieth Century and who criticizes the churchmen and their rituals which are, according to him, for their honors and not for Jesus the Crucified.

The Earth Gods (1931). Written shortly before he died, this book is a summary of Gibran's philosophy. He states that man is anxious to be nearer to the gods. In Gibran's philosophy, man is the food of the gods.

The Wanderer (1932). A posthumous publication which contains about fifty stories similar to those of Ebnel Mouqaffah and La Fontaine.

The Nymphs of the Valley (1948). It is a work similar to *Spirits Rebellious* in which Gibran attacks those who are in authority, whether civil or ecclesiastical, and who make laws and do not observe them. He ridicules law and traditions.

The Voice of the Master (1959). A collection of articles and essays on various topics, mainly on life and love and other interesting subjects.

Thoughts and Meditations (1961). *Spiritual Sayings* (1963).

These are two books containing a collection of his thoughts, sayings and spiritual considerations and thinking.

Self-Portrait (1960). A collection of his personal letters sent to different friends around the world.

GIBRAN'S FAME

Auguste Rodin in a book dedicated to his friend Henri Beaufort said that the world would expect much from the genius of Lebanon and declared that Gibran was "the William Blake of the Twentieth Century".[41] Arnold Bennett in *This is the United States of America* tells the Arabs that they have enough pride to have Gibran reminding the materialistic people of the United States of the Torah, the Psalms and the teachings of Christ.[42] Dr. William Guthrie, who entertained a profound faith in the mission of Gibran as a modern prophet, referred to the book *Jesus, the Son of Man* as 'The Gospel according to Gibran'.[43] And Arthur Berzbein goes as far as to say: "If I were one of the faithful who believe in the second return of Christ, I would believe that he came in the person of Gibran".[44] President Wilson said as he greeted Gibran: "You are the first Eastern storm to sweep this country, and what a number of flowers it has brought."[45] Dr. Charles Fletcher wrote of him saying that Gibran's pen and brush revealed the most precious thing that his generation has offered to the American nation.[46] Claude Bragdon expressed his admiration in these words: No one deserves so well to be called philosopher, poet, painter, nobleman, as he whom the United States has lost in the person of Gibran, and the light which shines through his lines comes from Lebanon.[47] The American writer Barbara Young in *This Man From Lebanon* considers Gibran's thoughts as being as holy as those in the Holy Scripture.[48] *The Prophet* made such an impact in the United

29

States that Mrs. Douglas Robinson, sister of President Roosevelt, offered a grand banquet in honor of Gibran.

Barbara Young reports that at St. Mark's in-the-Bowery, New York, an adaptation of *The Prophet* is given every year as a religious drama. The same church has a vesper service at which the entire office is 'drawn from the rhythms of Khalil Gibran, poet-prophet of Lebanon.' These practices were initiated by Dr. William Guthrie. The National Catholic Reporter in its July 1968 issue reported that James Kavanaugh, the ex-priest, officiated at a wedding ceremony, and instead of Bible reading, he read verses from Gibran's *The Prophet*:

> Sing and dance together and be joyous but
> let each one of you be alone, even as the
> strings of a lute are alone, though they
> quiver with the same music.[49]

The Beirut Arabic daily *Al Nahar* reported in its issue of March 28, 1968, that a movie entitled *The Broken Wings* had been shown in New York with great success and is now being shown in various cities of the United States. It received a prize as "the best foreign movie" at the film festival of Sorrento, Italy.[50]

Recently, the writer was told by Brother Edward Baldwin, former novicemaster of the house of formation of the new members of the De La Salle Order, that his novices used to select Gibran's *The Prophet* as one of their favorite books for meditation.

Those few instances show the amount of popularity that Gibran enjoys throughout the world.

When at first we cast a glance at the works of Kahlil Gibran we get the impression that the material is quite limited in proportion to the world fame he enjoys. And the inquirer might ask: what are the reasons behind this disproportion?

It is quite simple. Gibran's fame comes from the fact that he wrote many things which were said by his predecessors concerning love, freedom, oppression, slavery and man-made laws. But the point which makes him appealing is that he attributes a touch of passing divinity to man and makes him feel the pinch and urge of love. For him love is "lord and master of us all; we are but obedient servants. Whoever disobeys love, disobeys God. For love is the only God." Freedom is above man-made laws, and a tyrant is a tyrant because he finds submissive people. The only law for him is his conscience which unites him to God. Happiness for him is never achieved without pain and suffering. Gibran seems to have a Nietzschean attitude in this respect, which also reflects upon Jesus whom he considered to be the Superman, a Superman who laughed and was above pain, and who was born naturally from a woman. He stripped Jesus of his divinity. Religion for him is a union with God which was quite above church laws. He attacked the people who wore gold rings and rich ornaments and who preached the Gospel without practising it. This stemmed out from his frustration during his early romance with Hala Dhaher, the girl he wanted to marry and who was then given to the bishop's nephew. In his life he witnessed also injustices done to people at the hands of the monks who according to him, were indirectly in collusion with local authorities.

The whole life and attitude of Gibran can be summed up as being a life of frustration stemming from his inability to liberate himself from man-made laws, and to liberate his brothers for whom he had a genuine compassion. His doctrine has something of mysticism, realism and hallucination. Although deep and quite fascinating in his exposé, he remains a man who had suffered much and who had tasted some happiness in his encounter with his fellow-men, with art, with women, with painting. He attributed to himself a kind of prophetic mission. He felt he was endowed to save his fellowmen from the slavery of man-made laws and advocated what he called 'the freedom of the children of God'.

If the reader is not aware of the reality of life and the destructive attitude of some points of his doctrine, he might get embezzled by Gibran's soft and thrilling way of saying things. Gibran's unique way of saying things and enveloping them in an aura of 'divine spirituality' is the key to his doctrine and fame. It is also fascinating to note the depth of his thinking and the mystic approach he has of life in general, especially for men who know how much love is really central to man's life and destiny.

MAJOR ARTISTIC INFLUENCES

Born in the high mountain regions of Lebanon, Gibran very early breathed the air of freedom, and learned to contemplate nature as found in the surrounding picturesque landscape. Hala Dhaher created the turmoil of happiness and pain in his heart. His contacts with monks who led a bourgeois life among the poor and who, according to him, imposed man-made laws on people's life,[51] gave rise to the bitterness he entertained against them and their teachings. The attempt of the bishop to snatch Hala, Gibran's sweetheart, from his heart and give her in marriage to his nephew[52] hardened him in his attitude.

In literature, he came under the influence of pre-Islamic authors such as Ebnel Muqaffah, Al Mutanabbi and a gallery of others whose portraits were painted by Gibran himself. They are displayed throughout his works. The more recent Arab writers also had their impact on him; among them was the Egyptian woman writer May Ziadeh who knew him mainly through his writings.[53] This clever and famous writer did not spare her criticisms on the problem of marriage and women's emancipation. She considered Gibran's position as "destructive to our society." Their friendship was so close that one day she received a letter from Gibran containing only the drawing of a burning heart pierced by a dagger.[54]

He knew two other modern Lebanese-American writers,

Ameen Rihani and Mikhael Naimy, both members of the literary Academy *Arrabitah* which Gibran founded in New York.[55] Mikhael Naimeh remained his closest friend until death. He even wrote at least two books about Gibran, *Kahlil Gibran: His Life and His Work*; and *Al Majmouat al Kamilat Li Mouallafat Joubran Khalil Joubran*, in which he reveals the personality of Gibran as no one else had done.

Gibran admired numerous western writers. We see throughout his writings the tremendous influence of Nietzsche and Dante as well as of André Gide. He wrote to Miss Watson saying that Nietzsche was the greatest mind ever produced.[56] In his paintings we see the influence of Auguste Rodin whom he knew and admired while he was in Paris. The painting of a burning hand with an eye in the center is the typical reproduction of Rodin's sculpture The Eye of God.[57] In his paintings we also notice the influence of classicism as well as of romanticism and expressionism. It is also evident throughout his works that he admired William Blake very much, and that he found in Blake's writings many of his own feelings and outlooks. Leonardo da Vinci and Botticelli were his masters in painting. When he was still eight he used to seclude himself in a room and gaze at their paintings for hours. He admired John Keats and read him widely. He was attracted especially by Keats' rich imagery and emotional appeal. He would even appropriate Keats' motto: "Write as epitaph on my tomb: 'Here lie the remains of the one who wrote his name in water.'" Like Keats he was a worshipper of beauty as well as of truth. This attitude is seen in his writings on Hala, the sweetheart whom he wanted to marry.[58]

Two women greatly influenced his life. Miss Mary Haskel first met him when she was viewing his paintings at an exhibit. She was unusually interested in them, became acquainted with Gibran and later on became his benefactress. The other woman, Miss Micheline, befriended him. Naimeh says that Gibran loved Micheline and even proposed that she be his mistress. She flatly refused.

33

Among the cities that influenced him was mostly Paris. Here he studied painting for three years at the *Académie Julien* and then at the *Beaux Arts,* and here he met a number of the great men of his generation, such as Henri de Beaufort, Debussy, the younger Garibaldi and Auguste Rodin. He spent more than twenty years in Boston and New York where he engaged in business, writing and painting. During his stay in the United States he kept to his Oriental habits of drinking heavy Turkish coffee, smoking native cigarettes and eating Lebanese food.

CHAPTER II

LOVE – A MANIFOLD AWAKENING

Love has always been a favorite and fascinating subject for philosophers, as well as for poets and writers. Some have added more confusion to its mystery; others have thrown further light, beclouded at the same time with errors and misconceptions.

To which group does Gibran belong? Aware of this state of confusion in which he also found himself, he starts a special essay on love and cautions that before speaking of love, he had purified his lips with a sacred fire. But he immediately adds "And when I opened my lips to speak you found me dumb."[1] Does he imply that when sacred fire had purified his lips he felt that love was so overwhelming a thing that he could not speak any more? It seems so, as another quotation affirms: "When I knew it (love), my words issued forth as a soft breath and the songs in my heart became a deep silence."[2] Before this, he could talk of love telling people what to do, but "when it invaded me, I asked for advice from anyone who was able to tell my heart about my heart and myself about myself."[3]

After such a state of self-oblation, what does he feel if he cannot talk of love? For him, love is a "flame consuming his heart, melting his emotions and passions." It is a "secret hand rough and sweet which takes hold of his soul in his loneliness and pours into his heart a drink in which bitterness and sweetness mingle." He describes the reactions he feels in a very Nietzschean manner, by saying that "he finds the sobs of love sweeter than laughter and happiness. It is a strange force that brings both death and life."[4]

He does not stop at that, but he wants to find an adequate explanation by asking himself "what is, then, that which we call love?" Gibran confesses his inability to answer and again asks people to explain this "mystery that stands behind the centuries, hidden in the conscience of our existence." Finally, he tries to use words just to add more confusion or to give an aura of greater mystery by asking whether "love is not behind the motivation of everything we do and the result of all the causes." For him it is an "awakening that has death and life, that generates a dream stranger than life and deeper than death." And he puts the question directly to his readers by asking them "who among us does not awaken from the stillness of life when love touches his soul with the tips of its fingers, and . . . cross valleys, and climb mountains to meet the woman he loves, and travel from afar to meet the beloved who is our life! . . ."[5]

Gibran, knowing the many sides of love, its sweetness and bitterness and the various attitudes that people take depending on their state, describes its meaning to persons of various ages and moods. For the old it is a "weakness inherited from our first parents." For the young it is "a decision that is part of our existence, which links our present with the past and the future," while for the tired woman it is "a deadly poison" and for the young, "is an elixir that is injected by the nymphs into the strong mind." "It is blind ignorance which starts in youth and ends in old age" for an old man. Another man with clear vision finds that it "is divine knowledge that makes us see things as the gods do" while it is a "thick cloud that envelopes the soul and hinders its existence"[6] for another.

Gibran ends his essay by relating what he himself heard from a voice from the temple: "life is divided into two; one half is frozen and the other half is burning, and love is that burning half."[7] Then Gibran went into the temple and knelt and prayed, asking the Lord to let him be the "food of flames and the food of this holy fire" which shows what Gibran really thinks of love; he is quite committed to it to the end, since he asks to be consumed by this divine flame that comes from the throne of "divinity."

These are the main lines of Gibran's doctrine of love. Now we shall examine them in detail.

THE "MYSTERIOUS CALL"

Gibran's mysticism goes deeper than that of the average writer; he speaks of love as being something beyond the understanding of man. The millions who are dazzled by his description of this "state of mystery" which practically every human being experiences must themselves feel living in a mysterious world of mysterious events surrounded by mysterious hands. Definitely Gibran does not share the opinion of Erich Fromm,[8] the modern outstanding psychoanalyst who says that love is an art that can be acquired through practice. Although Gibran does not object or reject the idea of a "development in love" he stressed clearly that love is a special mysterious and divine call.

> It is wrong to think that love comes from long companionship and persevering courtship. Love is the offspring of spiritual affinity and unless that affinity is created in a moment, it will not be created in years or even in generations.[9]

Gibran is convinced that love is not created by us, but is sent from above and directs everything the way it pleases. "Ere my soul preached to me, love was in my heart as a tiny thread fastened between two pegs."[10] Since he believes this, he even calls the person who loves "a plaything in the hands of love, knowing not where to go and what to do." Love embraces the whole being in a very indefinite way.

> Love has become a halo whose beginnings is
> its end, and whose end is its beginning. It
> surrounds every being and extends slowly to
> embrace all that shall be.[11]

We notice the contradiction of "beginning and end" and this "halo"; it is his typical manner of expressing the vagueness and mystery of things. He seems to be a phenomenologist *par excellence* who stops at appearances and finds satisfaction in what he thinks is a mystery. This is typically Oriental and often obscure to the western mind. It seems that Gibran stresses so much this "mysterious call" in order to let people know that their language is different from that of love. He warns them in a very blunt way by saying that this language is not for them and even what he writes is not for them. He also adds that these pages may be understood, but that the shadowy meanings which are not clothed in words and do not appear on paper, cannot be grasped. He finally asks what human being has never sipped the wine of the cup of love.[12]

It also seems that Gibran does not make much of a distinction between the heaven of theology and that of the cosmos. In Oriental literature and colloquial language the word "Alsamaa" is used indiscriminately for either which in turn has a touch of mysticism, poetry and divinity. In many mythologies the stars and the planets were supposed to be the seat of the gods. That is why we find the following description of love in one of his letters to Ameen Ghuraeb of March 28, 1908:

> They (lines of the letter) were written with
> the finger of the soul and the ink of the heart

upon the face of love that hangs between the earth and the stars and hovers between the East and West.[13]

But does this poetic language mean that Gibran does not consider all the theological aspects of love? It seems to the writer of this paper that Gibran being both a poet and mystic clothes his thoughts in very poetic language, but in the depths of his heart he seems to be thinking of both the poetical heaven of literature and the heaven of theology. We can conclude that this idea of love for which every human being strives and anticipates with great expectation, will continue to remain an unsolved mystery.

THE "SACRED FLAME"

As presented earlier, although Gibran's style is poetical it has theological depth. For instance, he says: "When you love you should not say 'God is in my heart'; but rather 'I am in the heart of God.' "[14] This passage shows clearly that Gibran's idea of divinity is genuine and not merely poetical. Between divinity, mystery and sacredness there is not much difference for lay people. What is divine remains practically a mystery, while sacredness seems to take another form of being beyond man-made laws. That is where Gibran wants to arrive in his doctrine of considering love as sacred and divine. He considers the laws imposed on marriage as man-made laws and therefore invalid as far as marriage is concerned. This attitude developed as a consequence of the marriage deals practiced in the East at that time, where marriage brokers were still powerful. Hence they mercilessly imposed marriage in which love was not present. The right of choosing a partner was denied to women. Their life was miserable from beginning to end. That is one of the

reasons why Gibran attacks man-made laws and considers
them as being against the essence of love which is divine
and which nobody can interfere with. In his story *Wardeh
Al Haneh* who was forced to marry Rashid Nu'man he takes
the girl as his mouthpiece to declare the sacredness of love:

> I prayed in the silence of the nights
> before Heaven, asking it to create in
> my soul a spiritual affinity that would
> draw close to me the man who had been
> chosen for my husband. But Heaven did
> not so, for love descends on our spirits
> on God's command and not on man's asking. . . .
> Then one black day I looked beyond the
> darkness and saw a soft light shining
> from the eyes of a youth who walked the
> highways of life alone and who dwelt alone
> among his books and papers in this poor
> house. I closed my eyes that I might not
> see those rays, and said within myself:
> 'Thy lot, O spirit, is the blackness of
> the tomb; covet not, therefore, the light!
> Then I listened and heard a divine melody,
> the sweetness of which made a trembling
> in my limbs, whose purity possessed my
> being . . . I closed my eyes not to see, but
> my eyes saw the light while they were yet
> closed and my ears heard the melody
> even though they were stopped.[15]

When Wardeh ran away from the husband who had been
forced upon her, she felt herself as being led by a sacred
and divine force:

> I was a harlot and a faithless woman in
> the house of Rashid Nu'man because he
> made me the sharer of his bed by virtue

40

of tradition and custom rather than as
a wife before Heaven, bound to him by
the sacred law of love and the spirit.[16]

This sacredness of love is often mentioned as being the
result of a direct intervention from God. When Gibran talks
to his beloved Halah Karameh he tells her that it is the hand
of God that brought their souls together before birth, and
made them prisoners of each other during all the days and
nights.[17] This sacredness is also extended to everything in
nature; therefore all the laws that govern the universe are
sacred and divine. He talks of the emotions that shook their
hearts, and calls them also "laws of nature similar to those
that guide the moon around the earth and the sun around
God."[18]

A sort of reincarnation is noted in Gibran's teaching on
love. He finds that the real consolation for true lovers who
have this sacred love is "to meet again in an immortal
union." He says it to his beloved Selma Karameh in a mood
quite similar to the Canticle of Canticles: "Love, my beloved Selma, will stay with me to the end of my life, and
after death the hand of God will unite us."[19]

In the story of *The Bridal Couch* the bride who ran away
from the husband who had been forced on her to follow
the one who was given to her by her "sacred feelings," and
who slew herself after slaying him, asked the audience in a
dramatic voice, to look so that "perchance you will see God's
face reflected in our faces and hear His sweet voice rising
up from our hearts." The story is quite dramatic and frightening. But Gibran remains logical with himself and with
his doctrine of "burning love which directs our course." He
shows clearly what he means when he says that love "cannot be resisted." He even calls it a "precious treasure, God's
gift sent to sensitive and great spirits."[20] This love besides
being sacred, divine and irresistible, is for the lover "an
arrow of fire with its special message unknown to the average
person." Gibran himself speaks of the experience he en-

41

countered when he saw Maryam whom he loved madly.
He confessed that "the waves of Maryam's being were lap-
ping the shores of my being, and I knew that the sacred
flame enveloping my heart had touched her heart."[21] For
Gibran, the bodily organ of the heart is still the symbol of
this romantic love which is mystically given to us by Heaven.
When the hand of a man touches the hand of a woman they
both touch the heart of eternity.[22] Many other passages carry
this same mystic-divine relation between two persons taken
up into the consuming fire of love. Gibran complains about
the poverty of human knowledge to express all the details
of this exchange between the two hearts. Here, he reminds
us of Bergsonian philosophy which advocates that the stream
of consciousness cannot be explained adequately by our
human language.[23]

THE LIGHT AND THE FLOWER

If Gibran's doctrine on love needed an outside element
to vivify the intensity of this "burning fire" he would have
gone into the world of illogicality and destroyed his personal
belief with his own argument. But on the contrary, Gibran
finds in love a "self-consuming and self-nourishing fire"
when he says that warm hearts do not need outside heat.[24]
What kind of heat is he talking about? Is it transitory heat
which comes and goes like a flash in the pan, or a steady and
strong heat? The answer will come naturally from the
qualities he attributes to this heat. In fact, he says: "This
heat is as strong as death that changes everything."[25] In
The Prophet his mouthpiece Almustafa preached to the
public saying that "love gives naught but itself and takes
naught but from itself."[26] The idea of reward seems to be
contrary to his doctrine. The average person thinks of love
as being something rewarding to his own self; others even

go so far as to make love a kind of exchange which brings excitement and love adventures. This type of love is far from the Gibranian doctrine which advocates the complete independence of love in its self-immolation where selfishness does not have any place at all. "Love possesses not nor would it be possessed; for love is sufficient unto love," thus advocating the doctrine of the "self-consuming and self-nourishing" which is at the essence of his attitude. Does this mean that love is inactive? Not at all. Gibran gives love a strong role to play in the life of the subject, with always one vital condition: the subject must be worthy of this "divine call." Then love will "direct his course." Thus love's aim is to "fulfill itself." In case the victim of love "needs have desires," Gibran tells him to desire only that he be melted like snow and become like a running brook singing its melody to the night and to know the painful side of love which is found in too much tenderness." Gibran does not hide the other side of love. This seems to be cruel when he urges him "to be hurt, wounded and punished by your own understanding of love and then bleed willingly and joyfully."[28] This state of bliss and sorrow, with wound and punishment, ecstasy and a touch of divinity, should be "a spur to let you wake at dawn with a winged heart and give thanks for another day of loving" and in case there is a time for rest at noon's hour it should be used to "meditate love's enchantment" and then be grateful for this state of blessed crucifixion and even "pray for the beloved and sing a song of praise" to end the whole process.

He also compares love to a flower which is sown in the earth to blossom; the seed for love is a dream which will soar into the mysterious sky which will bring down to you your beloved.[29] This flower is also independent and has a heavenly aspect which makes him say that love is the only flower that grows and blossoms without the aid of seasons.[30] This independence does not mean that there will be no development and adaptation. Gibran even warns that "if it does not spring itself it will always be dying,"[31] which means that there should be a perpetual renewal of love and this is vital to its life.

What about the effect of love on human nature? Gibran says that it "is boundless and mystifying, freeing the subject from jealousy and it is never harmful to the spirit," which will fill the soul with bounty. This tenderness for Gibran will create "hope without agitating the soul, will change earth to paradise and life to sweet dreams." Love is also associated with light — a symbol of goodness with a touch of divinity — of which Gibran says that it is "a word of light, written by a hand of light, upon a page of light."[32] This poetic-mystical outlook of Gibran on love makes him an idol to everyone who is led and swayed back and forth by its mood and sweetness, as well as its suffering. And those who think that love will end after the years of youth are told that during their youth love will be their teacher; in middle age, their help; and in old age, their delight.[33] After this consolation given to those who think of love as being only for a few years, he insists on updating and constantly watching its development so that its consuming fire may be effective; otherwise, "his life remains like a blank sheet in the book of existence."

So, love has a quenchless desire of renewal, but at the same time an independence which is constant. If changes do occur, some day, they will come from man's needs and not from love. Love is like death. It changes everything without changing itself.

"STRONGER THAN LIFE AND DEATH AND TIME"

The story in which Gibran best shows the depth and strength of love is *Spirits Rebellious*. In *The Bridal Couch* the bride had just come from the Church ceremony with musicians and well wishers. The bride had been married against her will. Her lover Selim had been the victim of calumny. During the banquet, the bride sees Selim sitting in the corner, sad and meditative. She loved him so much that she could not resist the temptation of going with him to the garden, where she vowed her deep and strong love for him.

> I love you Selim as I love no other and
> I shall love you to the end of my days.
> They told me that you had forgotten me
> and abandoned me out of love for another.
> They poisoned my heart with their tongues
> and rent my breast with their claws and
> filled my soul with their lying . . . Najibeh
> played my feelings so that I might be sat-
> isfied with her kinsman as a husband; and
> it was so . . . but now I have come to take
> you in my arms, for there is no power in
> this world that can send me back to the
> embrace of a man whom I wed in despair . . .
> I have come to follow you to a far-off
> land, to the very ends of the jinn —
> yea — into the clutches of Death itself.[34]

Selim refuses to accept her offer because of the danger of dishonour and urges her to return to her husband. But the bride answers energetically that she would not return:

> even though I be at my last breath of
> life. I have left it (the house) for-
> ever . . . Behold my arms around your neck;
> no force shall lift them. My spirit had
> drawn near to your spirit, and death
> shall not let them part.[35]

But Selim refuses to let her leave her husband, so she

draws a dagger and buries it in his heart. The people, hearing screams, find the dying Selim. He murmurs:

> Death is stronger than life, but love is
> stronger than death . . . Let me kiss the
> hand that has broken my bonds. Kiss my
> lips, the lips that did take upon them
> lies and conceal the secrets of my heart . . .
> after my spirit has taken flight into
> space, put the knife in my right hand and
> say to them that he killed himself out of
> envy and despair.[36]

The lover places his hand over his pierced heart, his head falls to one side, and he dies.

The bride screams and calls on people to awaken, to hasten to her "for we shall reveal to you the secrets of love and death and life."[35]

> The bride continued to speak to the
> public: Draw near and tremble not because
> of this knife, for it is a sacred instru-
> ment that will not touch your unclean
> bodies and your black hearts. Gaze awhile
> on this comely youth adorned with the adorn-
> ments of marriage. He is my beloved and I
> have slain him because he is my beloved . . .
> You understand naught of my words, for the
> depths are not able to hear the song of the
> stars, but you shall tell your children of
> a woman who slew her lover on her wedding
> night.[38]

In that instant the bride lifts the dagger, thrusts it into her heart and falls beside her lover. Before giving up the spirit, she says: "You have waited for me, Selim, behold me here. I have broken the bonds and loosed the chains."

In *Thoughts and Meditations* under the heading of *"Union"* Gibran writes about the union that should exist among sister countries. While visiting a temple of the god Isis, he describes the strength of his love:

> "My love is as strong as your Pyramids,
> and the ages shall not destroy it. My
> love is as staunch as your Holy Cedars
> and the elements shall not prevail over
> it."[39]

In *The Prophet* when Almustafa, the chosen and the beloved, was on the point of leaving the city of Orphalese, the priests and the priestesses said unto him: "Much have we loved you. But speechless was our love, and with veils has it been veiled . . . and ever has it been that love knows not its own depth until the hour of separation.[40] The people had loved him and yet did not know the strength of their love for him until the time of departure. This is the case for each one of us when we depart from persons with whom we lived, wept and laughed.

In *Sand and Foam* Gibran contemplates on the strength of love which transforms everything: "When you reach the heart of life (which means here: love) you shall find beauty in all things, even in the eyes that are blind to beauty."

In *The Broken Wings* Selma loved Kahlil Gibran very much, but being betrothed to the bishop's nephew against her will, she keeps wishing for her lover. When the stillness of the night allows her to meet her lover, she describes the strength of love and its power over her: "Now I know that there is something higher than heaven and deeper than the ocean and stronger than life and death and time. I know now what I did not know before."[41] And Gibran, filled with emotion answers: "Selma became a supreme thought, a beautiful dream, an overpowering emotion living in my spirit."[42] When he gazed on her, he reached a state of happiness which he describes: "One look from a woman's eye makes you the happiest man in the world."[43] For Gibran, love is the only flower that grows and blossoms without the aid of seasons.[44]

When Gibran left Selma in the garden he felt that without love everything looked ugly and horrible. For him love is the true light that had showed him the beauty and wonder of the universe and "the eternal music I used to hear became a clamour, more frightening than the roar of a lion."[45] Love is the source of everything; in its presence everything is beauty; in its absence the whole world wears an ugly mask. Before leaving Selma, he said that "an hour passed, every minute of which was a year of love."[46] In *Kahlil the Heretic* when he was disappointed he shouted "what things are these mysterious forces that make playthings of us?"[47] But the highest point of strength of love either in its cruelty or in its sweetness is shown in the story of the *The Cry of the Graves*. Here three persons were summarily condemned to death by the oppressive authorities; then the corpse of each one was taken by a person who had loved him. A young man came near the harlot's corpse, dressed her naked body, and dug her grave with his hands. He had loved the girl, but her parents were opposed to his marrying her; one day while he was talking to her secretly, he was accused of rape. Now he risks his life to express the love that had been in their hearts.

A girl appeared to take the corpse of the beheaded youth, she risked her life to dig his grave and bury him. She confessed later that he was the young man who had delivered her from shame; she was being carried by the Ameer's officer to be raped, and this young man had defended her.

A sickly-looking woman clothed in rags, climbed a tree and gnawed through the rope that held the corpse of the third man. She buried his corpse and planted a cross on the grave. When asked why she had buried a thief, she answered that he was her faithful husband and father of her five children. He had farmed the monastery's land all his life and received only a loaf of bread. After having become weak, he was dismissed by the monks and when all his efforts to bring bread for his children failed, he went at night to the convent vault for a basket of flour. He was caught, judged and sentenced to death. She came to show her love for her husband, who had been faithful to her and to their children until death.

Thus Gibran, in a dramatic way, shows the strength of love, whether it be cruel or sweet. He has a special gift of contrast in his stories.

THE SOUND OF SILENCE

Gibran does not believe that real love needs to be eloquent. When love visits a soul it enlightens its corners.[48] For him, the "heartbreak of love sings." This singing is the consolation of the soul and it leads to understanding things which are overshadowed by sorrow. This sorrow is deeper than love; in Gibran's words: "There is a sorrow deeper than love, loftier than knowledge, stronger than desire, and more bitter than poverty." This sorrow for Gibran is not eloquent, it "is mute and has no voice." In another place, he says that "the secret in singing is found between the vibration in the singer's voice and the throb in the hearer's heart" which gives an idea of how to communicate one's ideas and feelings without using words.

Gibran himself confesses to his bosom friend Mikhael Naimeh: "In my heart, Meesha (Russian word for Michael), there are shadows and images that sway, walk, and expand like mist, but I am unable to give them the form of words."[49] Which means that the heart's secrets are so complicated that he finds, like Bergson, that this area is beyond space and time and form. Human language is inadequate to express everything that this heart utters and feels. The real lovers start developing their love not in words but in quiet silence: "Two spirits . . . had attained understanding in silence and drawn near to the circle of light on high,"[50] he says in his famous essay *Kahlil the Heretic*. In *The Broken Wings* when he met Selma he said that they should both be silent, each waiting for the other to speak, because "speech is not the only means of understanding between two souls. It is not the syllables that come from the lips and tongues that bring hearts together."[51] The energy of healing love is strong in its mute attitude. As when two lovers meet after a long separation, words seem to hamper their communication and mutual understanding. So they remain silent, unable to say what they feel and what they want to say. Gibran felt this situation more than once mainly when he paid visits to Selma after he knew that she was compelled to be betrothed to the bishop's nephew whom she did not love. He describes one of the meetings:

> A look which reveals inward stress adds
> more beauty to the face, no matter how
> much tragedy and pain it bespeaks; but
> the face which in silence does not an-
> nounce hidden mysteries is not beautiful,
> regardless of the symmetry of its fea-
> tures. The cup does not entice our lips
> unless the wine's color is seen through
> the transparent crystal.[52]

Gibran returns often to silence the only language of love in certain circumstances and writes:

> Look at me, my friend; study my face
> and read in it what you want to know
> and what I cannot recite. Look at me,
> my beloved . . . Look at me, my brother.[53]

But he sometimes opts for a manner of expression suited

to circumstances as the only way to communicate; thus he says that "when life does not find a singer to sing her heart, she produces a philosopher to speak her mind."[54] Therefore Gibran does not rule out any sort of communication, but he insists that in many difficult circumstances the best expression of love is silence which very often reflects either anguish or an overwhelming happiness. To consider that the eloquence of superfluous artificial words is necessary for love, is completely rejected by Gibran as senile.

A "BLESSED CRUCIFIXION"

While Gibran visited Selma, he was sorrowful because of the difficulties in their love affair. As soon as he touched her hand, he said that it was like a white lily and "a strange pang pierced my heart."[55] He then calls his meeting a drama witnessed by heaven. In *Spiritual Sayings* he calls love a "trembling happiness."[56] But in some of his other works such as *Thoughts and Meditations* in the story of *The Return of the Beloved,* when a girl approaches her slain lover, her hand trembled when it touched the edge of the scarf tied by loving fingers around the arm of the hero, now lifeless. In other passages he insists on the cruelty of love and calls it savage because it plants a flower and uproots a field; revives us for a day and stuns us for an age.[57] He seems to imply that love is revengeful. With one hand it offers pleasure and with the other sorrow and bitterness, which means that love is sorrow, and sorrow is love. In *Sand and Foam* he feels compelled to confess: "Strange the desire for certain pleasure is a part of my pain."[58]

It is of common knowledge and experience that the separation of lovers is one of the most cruel experiences in life. Gibran describes an experience he had with Selma. After a period of courtship, he travelled to Boston and there he was terribly upset by her failure to write. He complained of it in his letters to his friends. In *The Broken Wings* he becomes more explicit when he says that "his hopes were buried in the seas" and on this spot 'I lost my happiness, drained my tears, and forgot to smile."[59] He says clearly that love is embittered by passion; and he finds life hard and meaningless for a person away from his beloved, especially for a person who asks for love and receives passion.[60] By "passion", Gibran seems to mean the suffering side of love. In other passages he calls love "quenchless". When he writes to Ameen Guraieb on March 28, 1908, from Boston, he tells him that love and longing are the beginning and the end of our deeds.[61] In the story *The Last Watch*, the hero complains that those who turned from him did so on account of the over-abundance of love and their preference to drink from a cup rather than from a surging river. This symbolizes fiery, passionate and unlimited love that consumes and directs mercilessly the course of life.[62] In *The Last Watch*, Gibran lets his "Forerunner" speak as his mouthpiece and utters some of the best contrasts of love and pain. The *Forerunner* speaks of "love that lashed itself, of pride half-slain," and accuses his audience of loving the sword that strikes them and the arrow that seeks their breasts. He ends by telling them that "it comforts them to be wounded and only when they drink of their own blood can they be intoxicated."[63] Gibran shows great insight into human nature. Many people seek the sorrow of love and the intoxication and quenchless demands of its passion. Yet, despite it all they are happy and Gibran is one with them. He discloses not only his own love for them but also his own sorrow and pain: "Thus while my heart, bleeding within me, called you tender names."[64]

The powerlessness of the heart to do what it wants is also a sorrow for Gibran. He says that love wants to burn, consume itself and fulfill its promises, keep its word, but alas the heart will bleed because of its weakness: "How shall the heart of a fruit be stretched to envelop the fruit also?" O my faith I am in chains . . . and I cannot fly with you."[65] "Yet out of my heart you rise skyward, and it is my heart that holds you, and I shall be content."[66]

Gibran everywhere seems to be resigned to the fate of love and to remain logical to his doctrine, i.e., that love directs our course and that our interference is a cause of more frustration and agony. He believes like Bergson that man is a prisoner of time and circumstances. All he asks of his love is to feel with him, to have faith and to hear his complaints.[67] Elsewhere he consoles his lover: "every now and then we could calm and wipe our tears and start smiling, forgetting everything except love."[68] With a kind of resignation to the cruelty and sweetness of love, Gibran writes, "love kills my desires so that you may live freely and virtuously. False love or limited love, asks for possession of the beloved, but real or unlimited love asks only for itself."[69] Does he imply here that where there is real love, there is real freedom for the lover? This is uncertain. In another passage in his writings he says that "love is the only freedom in the world because it so elevates the spirit that the laws of humanity and the phenomena of nature do not alter its course."[70] It must be clear to the reader that Gibran's subtle vocabulary and its oriental exaggeration make it difficult to see his real stand and his real theory on love and sorrow. A more detailed analysis of Gibran's personality is necessary to assess the issue.

"BRINGS LAUGHING AND REJOICING"

Gibranism cannot accept the idea that love can exist in the heart with doubts or suspicion. In *Sand and Foam* Gibran states that love and doubt have never been on speaking terms.[71] In other words, when love unites two hearts there should be no secrets or double-dealing. This frankness and readiness to be open does not mean that it is possible to know everything. Secrets unknown and buried in the depth of the heart will still remain secrets but there will always be a kind of understanding of these secrets as Gibran puts it in seemingly contradictory terms when he says: "Only those with secrets in their hearts could divine the secrets in our hearts."[72]

Very often people in love think that embracing is a way of experiencing pleasurable emotional sensations or thrills. Gibran takes a different view. When lovers embrace, he thinks that they do not embrace each other, but rather embrace what is between them.[73] What is then the result of this intimate gesture? The lover's fingers and caresses are the way to understanding, to soothe the pains of the day and the violence of life. When this is done, the real embrace will "bring laughing and rejoicing." This reminds the reader of the basic meaning of love which is a "burning flame, self-consuming and self-nourishing" which recurs again and again in Gibran's writing.

"OUR PLEASANT SWOON"

Gibran finds that nothing is more beautiful in life than being with one's beloved. He experienced this more than once when he met his beloved Selma. At one of these meetings, Selma's father came in after speaking to the bishop's nephew; he told them of the arrangement and they were "awakened from our pleasant swoon and plunged from the world of dreams into the world of perplexity and misery."[74] He contrasts the joy of the days when he met his beloved with those nights of sorrow when he was not with her; "nothing was more beautiful than those days of love,

54

and nothing was more bitter than those horrible nights of sorrow."[75] It might seem strange that Gibran who finds pain and sorrow in love, talks of happiness. He sees clearly both the happiness experienced in love and the sorrow that necessarily accompanies it. With love he finds not only happiness but also freedom where his mind can fly in the spacious firmament. The heart is the dwelling of the beloved and out of it his beloved rises skyward and this same heart holds her and with her it shall be content. This is why he cannot find how it is possible for real love to be enchained by any man-made laws. He places on love the crown of sacredness, of silence, of understanding and of happiness joined to freedom, which takes him skyward to live with the angels and the stars. In other words, it transports him into a world unknown to those who have not felt the magic call of this mysterious love that brings freedom and happiness to man's heart.

Chapter III

BEAUTY — THE HOLY RAY

Very often beauty is relative. Differences of artistic tastes varying from one culture to another are tangible proofs of this. Gibran seems to make a correlation between beauty and love. This may seem quite natural to us; for him there is something deeper and more meaningful.

That beauty and love are interrelated, Gibran shows in many passages. For him to go to the Louvre and stand before the paintings of Raphael, da Vinci and Corot "is quite inspiring to man's heart, who would then be able to write about beauty and love."[1] He states defiantly that in the past, "kings and sultans received from us reverence and admiration, but that today we follow only beauty and love."[2]

What is real beauty for Gibran? Is it necessarily based on physical aspect? In a number of passages, he says that beauty depends on the spiritual accord between a man and a woman,[3] and not necessarily on the physical features of the body. This does not mean that physical beauty does not exist. As stated earlier, Gibran attaches much importance to the spiritual aspect of beauty and the spiritual is not understood by everyone:

Only our spirits can understand beauty,
or live and grow with it. It puzzles
our minds; we are unable to describe it

in words; it is a sensation that our eyes
cannot see, derived from both the one who
observes and the one who is looked upon.
Real beauty is a ray which emanates from
the holy of holies of the spirit, and
illumines the body as life comes from the
depths of the earth and gives colour and
scent to a flower.[4]

THE "INTERNAL REFLECTION"

Gibran positively says that beauty is increased by our
attitudes. He illustrates this by describing his emotions
during his meetings with Selma. Each one of us is aware
that it is only after communicating with a person that the
beloved becomes attractive and little by little more and
more attractive. Then the "crush" comes and the tornado
of "I am in love with her," starts governing the ego. Then
the more visits one makes, the more flame and effect they
give to beauty and love.

In the case of Gibran's visits with Selma, "every visit
gave me a new meaning to her beauty and a new insight
into her sweet spirit,"[5] until she became to him like a book
whose pages he could understand and whose praises he
could sing, but which "I could never finish reading." The
last passage is most significant. Why does he say he could
not finish reading the book? Obviously because the deeper
his admiration for her, the deeper his attraction became.
A woman, he continues, whom Providence has provided
with beauty of spirit and body is a truth, at the same time
both open and secret, which could be understood only by
love and can be touched only by virtue; and when we
attempt to describe such a woman she disappears like a
vapour.[6] This passage reveals the keynotes of Gibran's

understanding of beauty. He connects it with the spirit as well as with the body. He attributes it to Providence and he claims that we can understand it only by love and touch it or more correctly, possess it physically or psychologically, by virtue and not by lust and licence. Gibran's attitude toward love, in this connection at least, is highly spiritual and fascinating, and offers itself as a model to people of our generation.

For Gibran, Selma was the ideal woman who revealed everything to him. Her face was like a mirror. He says that no words can describe its expression which reflects internal suffering, then heavenly exaltation.[7] Here again he talks about physical features which are completely dominated by the "internal reflection" of her soul. He also attributes to Selma his ability to "worship beauty by the examples of her own beauty",[8] a statement that corroborates an earlier statement, namely, that beauty is increased and made "more beautiful," by mutual attention throughout the period of courtship.

"Silence, love, beauty and virtue dwell together" according to Gibran and he found them in Selma when he visited her.[9] This collection of qualities impressed Gibran so much that he labels them as beauty which was erected by the four qualities that love had blessed, in which "the spirit could worship and the heart kneel to pray."[10] This means that a whole atmosphere of heavenly aura reigns in the heart of this idol that was created by the imagination, the mind and Providence. It is haloed beauty which is for Gibran the holy of holies of man's happiness and bliss in this world and which has to be continued at a higher degree in the second.

CHAPTER IV

WOMEN – THE LIGHT
UNTO THE LAMP

In general, when Gibran speaks of love, he means possession by the heart of affection, compassion and sympathy. But in many places he definitely means the love between man and woman. In Arabic there is a special word for each type of love; in general, the word *"hob"* is used to mean "like" as well as "love." As we shall be dealing with Gibran's concept of woman in the world of love, it seems fitting to consider briefly the many women who influenced Gibran's life.

Gibran recognized that women in general were very influential on him, starting with his mother, sister and girl friend. He writes:

"I am indebted for all that I call "I" to
women, ever since I was an infant. Women
opened the windows of my eyes and the doors
of my spirit. Had it not been for the
woman-mother, the woman-sister, and the
woman-friend, I would have been sleeping
among those who seek the tranquility of the
world with their snoring."[1]

Does Gibran mean here a biological necessity or a physical dependence? It does not seem so. He means the psy-

chological role that a woman plays in man's life. This starts
in childhood and should blossom into real love in marriage.

While in Boston he fell into the hands of a wicked woman,
thirty years of age, who led him astray.[2] Because of this
misadventure his mother sent him back to Lebanon under
the pretense of studying Arabic in Beirut.

In his late teens, while he was visiting his village he fell
in love with a girl of the best family of his village, the
Dhahers. When he asked for her hand, her parents refused
to grant his request. When he sought the help of the parish
priest he was told flatly, "Who are you to marry the daughter
of the Dhahers? You are a commoner. You are mad."[3] This
rebuff brought his first bitterness. Henceforth, he entertained a low idea of bargained marriage, which he later
savagely attacked in the story of Selma Karameh.

During an exhibit of his paintings in Boston, he made the
acquaintance of a Miss Haskel who took a special interest
in his painting and promised to help him. Their friendship
lasted many years. She encouraged him to exhibit his works
in Paris where she had acquaintances at a school of arts.
The directress, Miss Emily Micheline, liked Gibran's works,
gave him advice and her friendship.

In Boston, he met an American woman writer, who influenced his life. Unfortunately, her name remains unknown
to us.

He was befriended by the famous Egyptian woman writer,
May Ziadeh, who continued correspondence with him oc-
casionally and giving him criticism and advice. It is worth
noting that Miss Ziadeh did not accept his teaching that
"marriage must be freed from man-made laws which will
otherwise destroy society."

These contacts with women necessarily influenced Gibran.
It is not surprising that he had a very friendly attitude toward women, because he received material as well as psy-
chological help from them. "A woman is to a nation what
light is to a lamp."[4] He places woman on the summit of the
world. She illumines the world. She seems to be responsible

for man's genius and achievement. We all know that great men, including statesmen, were generally influenced by the women in their lives. So Gibran compares woman to light.

For Gibran, "every man loves two women; the one is the creation of his imagination, and the other is not born."[5] This seems to be a puzzling statement. What does he really mean? Does he imply that in practice we love, not what we find in a woman but what our imagination creates for us? This seems to be so. Gibran is always the victim of his imagination. His happiness as well as his bitterness is the work of his imagination as is very often the case for each of us. This non-existent woman that Gibran thinks we love, could be the idealistic person whom we cannot find in this world of limited response to the mind and spiritual elan.

Another amazing contradiction is found in one of his statements in a letter sent to his friend May Ziadeh where he complains about his own situation between two women who are for him like two lamps and he says:

> What shall I tell you about a man whom God
> has arrested between two women, one of whom
> turns his dream into awakeness, and the
> other his awakeness into dream?[6]

Gibran says that the first Eve led Adam out of Paradise by her own will, while Selma, the girl he loved, made him enter willingly into the paradise of pure love and virtue by her sweetness. But Gibran does not stop at that. He goes on to say that what happened to the first man happened to him also, meaning that Selma was the occasion of his being forced out of the Paradise of love without having disobeyed any order.[7] Gibran believes that men who have not tasted life's truths do not know the meaning of a woman's agony when her spirit stands between the man whom Heaven has willed her to love and the man to whom the laws of his fellows have bound her.[8] Gibran refers here to the suffering of a woman when she is compelled to marry

63

a man whom she does not love or who has been imposed on
her.

SECRETS OF THE HEART

Gibran states that understanding is a condition for happiness. "He who would understand a woman . . . is the very
man who would wake from a beautiful dream to sit at a
breakfast table."[9] For himself he confesses that he loved
the woman of his heart in understanding while the other
woman of restless nights he loved in pity.[10] For him the
woman he loved had her cup ever full which means having
a limitless source of consolation and response to man's love.
The first love is usually the one that keeps coming back to
man's mind throughout life. Gibran says that he tries to
recapture that strange hour, the memory of which charges
his deepest feelings and makes him happy in spite of all
the bitterness of its mystery.[11] Selma was Gibran's first love.
For him she will live forever. Her memory brings back both
happiness and bitterness. Gibran sums up his thoughts by
saying that in every young man's life there is a "Selma" who
appears to him suddenly in the spring of life, transforms his
solitude into happiness and fills the silence of his night with
music.[12] Does this mean that it is impossible for man to
leave one love for another without recalling the first love?
That is what Gibran seems to imply, but we do not find an
answer to the question as to whether it is possible to love
truly another woman whom we meet later on in our life
and to forget all about the first. Gibran writes subjectively
on account of his blind love for Hala Dhaher, but this is
not necessarily true for everyone.
Gibran states clearly that he loved his beloved with understanding as stated above, but he blames poets and writers
for failing to understand the reality of woman, the hidden

secrets of her heart.[13] He attributes this to their looking at her through the veil of sex which is only the external attraction,[14] and finding nothing except weakness and submission. Gibran found in woman a cup overfull of love which brought happiness but also bitterness to his life.

A woman's heart is totally different from a man's. Gibran says ironically that "many a woman borrows a man's heart; very few could possess it," which means that a woman can behave like a man for a time but not for always.

ONE LOOK, ONE TOUCH, ONE KISS

Gibran is rather insistent on the spiritual aspect of love. He never mentions the physical satisfaction of petting, which is a trap for men in general. He stresses the power of a glance when he says: "One look from a woman's eye makes you the happiest man in the world."[15] It is true that a glance from a person may reveal the hidden secrets of his heart. All love songs mention that the eyes are the mirror of the soul and the heart. With one look a woman can hypnotize a man and win him over. One glance from a man can have a tremendous influence on a woman, and win her trust and affection. In other passages he says that his greatest desire was merely to "behold the light of her eyes and hear the music of her voice." By voice here he does not mean so much what she says as how she speaks. We see that he stresses the effect that the sound of a voice has on him. Logical and cohesive thinking he does not expect from a woman, as he says ironically in another passage: "Listen to the woman when she looks at you, but not when she talks to you."[16] "When two women talk they say nothing; when one woman speaks she reveals all of life."[17] In her face is in general the expression of a woman's hidden secrets. When he was talking to Selma and she knew that she could not

65

marry him, her face clouded and showed distress which Gibran describes. "All these changes I saw in Selma's face, but to me they were like a passing cloud that covered the face of the moon and made it more beautiful." A look which reveals inward stress adds more beauty to the face, no matter how much tragedy and pain it bespeaks; but the face which in silence does not announce hidden mysteries is not beautiful, regardless of the symmetry of its features.[18] Gibran implies that the physical features are not important. What is important is the expression that gives a clear and revealing picture of the heart. He likens the face to a glass of wine which does not attract our lips unless the wine's colour is seen through the transparent crystal.[19] The hands are for him a symbol of the love a woman has for a man, which can electrify and make him the happiest man in the world. "Her hand was still on my head as she spoke, and I would not have preferred a royal crown or a wreath of glory to that beautiful smooth hand whose fingers were twined in my hair."[20] This has the effect of melting two hearts and making them one, the essence of love. He confesses it when he says that moment became dearer than a friend and closer than a sister and more beloved than a sweetheart. "She became a supreme thought, a beautiful dream, an overpowering emotion living in my spirit."[21] Finally, the highest form of affection is the kiss which a man receives from a woman. When Gibran kissed Selma's hand he said: "The memory melts my heart and awakens by its sweetness all the virtue of my spirit."[22]

In the various instances in his life, Gibran reveals many other aspects of woman which he associates with love. Let us mention the case of the death of Selma. Gibran erected a tomb in Beirut, then wrote: "My beautiful one is dead and nothing is left to commemorate her except my broken heart and a tomb surrounded by cypress trees. That tomb and this heart are all that is left to bear witness to Selma." In other passages he even asks all those who come to Beirut to visit the tomb of the woman who stole his heart, and to lay a wreath of flowers on it.

The various stories he relates are mainly of women who were compelled to marry men not of their choice, which led many of them either to take their life or to follow their true lover. We have in mind *The Bridal Couch.* The victim, on her marriage night, left her husband and ran away with her heart's desire. When the latter was afraid of accepting her love, she stabbed him and then stabbed herself with the same dagger, so that she might join him in immortal love beyond the grave.

In *The Cries of the Graves,* three stories reveal the attachment a woman can have to her loved one. After his execution, the slain hero's beloved risked her life to dig a grave and bury him. The wife of the poor man who was executed for taking a basket of flour from the convent buried him at the risk of her life out of love.

Gibran complains about the slavery of Oriental womanhood on account of arranged marriages. He blames men who despise the sterile woman because as he puts it she "is looked upon with disdain everywhere because of most men's desire to perpetuate themselves through posterity." Gibran also says that in some instances, the reward of the love of a woman is suffering when she does not find the right man, that is, the one who does not seek glory and reputation.[23] In some other stories, he goes so far as to justify a woman's divorcing her "false husband," that is, the one who was forced on her. But Gibran does not want men to pity women; he considers that pity belittles them. He accuses those who impute to women the evils of society of being oppressive to her. He praises the man who accepts her as made by God, and says that he alone does her justice.[24]

Does Gibran mean on the whole that a woman does not have faults like other human beings? Not at all. He feels that the love God has planted in her is also a source of destruction to her and to man.[25] Gibran is not blind to woman's faults. He asks men to forgive her faults if they want to en-

67

joy her great virtues.[26] Moreover, psychology tells us that real understanding between husband and wife results from acceptance of each other's weaknesses and human frailty. That is what Gibran means.

The problem of the ugly woman is also dealt with. Referring to the instance in which a man married a woman for her wealth and later on left her on account of lack of love and attraction, Gibran says that "she finds nothing except the glance of her reflection in the mirror."[27]

We find only a single instance in which he refers in the same story to another lady, "cold of face and ugly of soul"[28] who was accepted by a rich man. When he dies, she took his wealth and led a life of shame. In another passage, cited earlier, Gibran hints that the beauty of the face lies in the eyes, independently of the "symmetry of features," which probably means that an ugly woman can be attractive and lovable despite her features.

"I MYSELF AM A PROBLEM"

Once Gibran was invited to a party by an American lady. When he came, he found that he was the only guest. After inquiry about this strange circumstance, the lady told him that they would be the only people present at the party, and that they would enjoy it very much. When Gibran heard that, he promptly turned and left the house.[29]

Does this incident mean that Gibran did not appreciate marriage, that he liked to be free to "enjoy" himself without the responsibility of parenthood? One answer is found in an instance reported by Jaber in his book *Joubran* when he says that one day Gibran was talking to himself saying: "How is it possible for an artist to be faithful to one woman, when he is impressed by a constantly renewed love?"[30] It seems that Gibran was deeply attracted to women in a physical way, and that he thought it would be impossible for him to be faithful to one since he found beauty in so many other women too.

We find another instance in which some American ladies asked him why he did not get married. He answered that he gets so absorbed into his work that he forgets all about women and love, and that he would be sorry for the woman he would marry. It appears then that Gibran avoided marriage on account of his career. Perhaps he had sexual relations with some women since he confesses to Micheline that he would like her to be his mistress. She refused bluntly.

> Ah, Kahlil, Kahlil! I'm willing to be the
> mat under your feet and the dust on your
> sandals. I'm happy to be your servant —
> to wash your clothes, to sweep and dust
> your room, to cook your meals, to prepare
> your coffee, but not to be your mistress."

To which Gibran retorted that this was a "sacrilege against both life and love," He told Micheline not to separate what God had joined together and said that it is love that binds and unbinds. He then refers to the word "mistress."

> Mistress? Many a mistress is nobler in
> the eyes of life than thousands of wives
> whose ties to their mates have been sanc-
> tified by the laws of the earth but con-
> demned by the laws of heaven. Love is
> absolute. It is a law unto itself."

From this quotation we find that Gibran loved Micheline and wanted to take her as his mistress, putting in practice his doctrine that "love is that what unites man to woman," without official marriage ceremony.

But Gibran also confessed to Micheline that there was another woman in his life called Mary. But he made this confession out of sorrow for Micheline after he had lied to her about a woman in his life, who had paid for his studies in Paris. But his relations with her had been limited to accepting her money:

> "Yes, I have sinned against you and myself,
> Micheline, when I allowed another woman to
> share my life with you, profiting by her
> purse and mind while taking freely of your
> heart, and flesh and blood. I lied to you
> when you asked me of the woman and that I
> had arranged for a loan from some relatives
> and friends. Your sensitive heart felt that
> woman's presence, and it gave the lie to my
> tongue. How I wish I had declared all things
> to you. . . . Ah, come Micheline! Come to me,
> soul of my soul and heart of my heart. . . . I
> am ready to make amends. Come! Else I'll
> pluck you out of my heart even if my own
> heart be plucked in the painful operation."[31]

Gibran did not succeed in making Micheline his mistress. He had high regard for William Blake's wife, whom he admired very much as a beautiful, understanding woman. He wished to marry Mary even though she was ten years his senior and there was no physical attraction.

> What if there be no attraction between her
> body and mine as such as that which exists
> between my body and Micheline's? It is
> enough that our souls feel that attraction.
> Yes, I should marry her, and the two of us
> should live a clean married life. I shall
> be happy when they say about me what they
> said of Blake: "He is a madman. Madness
> in art is creation. Madness in poetry is
> wisdom. Madness in the search for God is
> the highest form of worship."[32]

From all these instances and quotations it does not seem to us clear if Gibran spoke of sexual relations in speaking to Micheline "of taking freely of your heart, and flesh and blood." But what is clear is that Gibran believed in the right to have a mistress, thus bypassing the laws of legal marriage, advocating that love is the only criteria for taking a woman as a mistress.

But we know that Gibran was trying to be chaste in his life when he was expecting the visit of a Lebanese girl who praised his writings:

> "I am already a torch lighting the paths
> of people far away. I must be as people
> picture me to be — clean, upright, trans-
> parent, charitable, fair to the oppressed,
> hard on their oppressors, patient in pain,
> strong and above all lowly passions. Save
> me, Lord, from myself. Cleanse me of all
> my impurities. Forge me in the forge of
> Your Right."[33]

And when the girl knocked at his door he prayed in his heart saying: "God save us from the hour of temptation," which shows that Gibran was aware of the weakness of the flesh.

When he finally proposed to Mary Haskell, she asked him whether he was "clean." And Naimeh explains this question by saying that Mary "wished to know if he was free of ugly sexual diseases." But the question "turned him from a lamb into a wounded lion." Such a question was an insult to Gibran's pride, to hear Mary doubting his "cleanness." According to Naimeh, this question stopped Gibran from marrying Mary, an act which would have changed the course of his life; Naimeh says rightly that the old aphorism fits here: "Man proposes and God disposes."[34]

Chapter V

MARRIAGE – "STRINGS THAT QUIVER WITH THE SAME MUSIC"

We have seen the great importance that Gibran gives to real love between two persons which normally is a prelude to marriage. The history of man according to him is "birth, marriage and death."[1] Marriage seems to him to be the climax of love in this world, and therefore a very important step. It is of such importance that he calls marriage "either death or life";[2] there is "no betwixt and between."

In *The Prophet* he answers those who asked him to talk about marriage:

"You were born together and together you
shall be for ever more; you shall be together when the white wings of death
scatter your days. Aye, you shall be together even in the silent memory of God."[3]

Those who read all his works can be puzzled by his insistence on the unity and sacredness of marriage, while in other passages he seems to be in favor of divorce. True, he does not consider an artificial union of a couple as true marriage. As we have seen earlier, Gibran has a very noble and spiritual idea of love and marriage. In a sense, as N. H. Nahmad has put it in his introduction to *Spirits Rebellious*, he does not recognize divorce when there was a real union of love (if we rightly understand what he means by sacredness and unity):

Gibran seems to seek deliberately the
undermining of the very foundations of
established society as we know it and
to set at naught the sacredness of marriage vows. But in fact he is not doing so.[4]

This sacredness is stressed very much by Gibran almost
everywhere. He finds that there is a kind of sacredness in
marriage that cannot be taken lightly. But he also warns:
"Let there be spaces in your togetherness. And let the winds
of heaven dance between you." He probably means that when
you are together you should not let your love degenerate so
that you forget that you are sacredly united in the "heart
of God." He adds:

"Love one another, but make not a bond
of love: let it rather be a moving sea
between the shores of your souls. Fill
each other's cup but drink not from one
cup."[5]

These seemingly contradictory statements mean that love
should be mutual and not separate. In other words, love
should not be individual and selfish. He continues saying
that you should "give one another of your bread but not
eat from the same loaf"; meaning to say that love should be
varied and not limited to the same recipe; the imagination
should find ways and means to give variety to love. "Sing
and dance together and be joyous, but let each one of you
be alone." This seems to contradict the first statement, but
not in reality. He wants each to be free, and at the same time
to allow the other person to be free. The two must act together, while conserving their freedom. He compares this
to "strings of a lute that are alone though they quiver with
the same music." He continues to compare the place of each
individual in this unity, to the "pillars of the temple which
stand apart, and the oak tree and the cypress which grow not
in each other's shadow."[6]

74

The woman's love binds her spirit to that of her husband; she pours her love into his heart, and the two become one member in the body of life and one word on the lips of God.[7] Gibran keeps insisting on the unity of marriage; it binds two persons "in a single divine spirit in the two human bodies made beautiful by youth and clothed in unison." He even says that this unity is protected by God "from the anger and blame of people," and a complete and perfect understanding arises from their "transparent faces lighted by purity."

THE LIVING HELL

Let us first state what he means by marriage. In Gibran's opinion true marriage is contracted by mutual love whereas the unions arranged by marriage brokers according to customs and traditions are false. Very often wealth, power, reputation are the main bases for the deals.

Gibran makes clear in his numerous stories that marriage can be a hell for a person who is married against his will. The stories are usually taken from real life pointing to the miserable situation in which cruel customs and traditions can leave a person. The most salient stories are found in *Spirits Rebellious*.

In the story of Wardeh El Hani Gibran depicts an unhappy woman who has left her husband and his wealth to live in poverty with the man she loves. In this tale, Gibran seems deliberately to undermine the pillars of society.[8] He shows a girl being married against her will to an older rich man. There is no love between the two. When Wardeh El Hani leaves her husband to follow the one she loves, she is called an adulteress. Gibran comes to her defense by asking whether she would not commit a greater sin in sharing the life of a man she cannot love and accept as her true lover?[9]

The *Bridal Couch* is a tale of a wedding party that started in joy and ended in tragedy. It depicts the odd nineteenth-century custom of marriage arrangements in which the girl is the victim of a forced marriage often to a man she does not love.

The story tells how the bride, just before her marriage was consummated, slew her lover who was attending the feast and thrust the same dagger into her own heart. She lay near him so that she might rest with him and meet him in the next world, there to enjoy the love that the actual world and tradition denied her.[10]

In many other stories Gibran shows that arranged marriages often create a living hell. He says that a woman is unhappy who through her ignorance finds herself living with a man whom she does not love although he may give her many gifts, money and clothes. He is not able to touch her heart with the living flame of love, to satisfy her spirit with the divine wine that God makes to flow from a man's eyes into a woman's heart.[11]

In another story a woman complains of the shackles of custom binding her body before she knew the meaning of those bonds. Gibran adds that a woman's happiness is not in the glory and lordship of a man, neither is it in his generosity or kindness; but it is in a love that binds her spirit to his spirit, her heart to his heart, thus making the two bodies one in Life.[12] He does not want the woman to be looked upon as a commodity, purchased in one house and delivered to another, as it was the custom during the Victorian period and at the beginning of the twentieth century. He deplores the Oriental woman's situation and calls it slavery.[13] He says that the sorrow of the parents at the marriage of a daughter is comparable to their happiness at the marriage of a son, because the latter brings a new member into the family while the former loses a member.

As a logical conclusion to his thinking, he does not believe that a woman who has been forced to marry a man she does not love, should live with him until death. He has great sympathy towards her when she is forced to lead a life of unhappiness and constant frustration. He criticizes the people who call such an unfaithful woman an adulteress and a whore.[14] When the Ameer took the unfaithful woman in her nakedness, and then had her stoned by the multitude who afterwards praised him for his noble deed, Gibran adds: "The unfaithfulness of women is an abomination, but who has made the stoning of bodies pleasant?"[15] The story of the Beirut woman is proof of this sympathy towards divorce when a woman is forced into marriage against her will or when mutual love does not exist. He warns people against gossiping and has Wardeh El Hani say:

> Those people who gossip are like the de-
> serted caves of the valleys that throw
> back voices in echo without understanding
> their meaning; they know not of God's
> sacred law in His creatures; neither are
> they aware of the true faith. They know
> not when a man is guilty and when he is
> not, but rather do they look only at out-
> ward things, their weaksighted eyes not
> seeing what is concealed.[16]

How much does Gibran's argument favor the new outlook on marriage? The author does not know. It is worth mentioning that the Roman Catholic Church allows separation in cases of forced marriages.

Chapter VI

PAIN AND SORROW –
THE AGONY OF THE ECSTASY

In a letter to his bosom friend, the Lebanese philosopher Mikhael Naimeh, he describes the mingling of pain and sorrow and even confusion in his heart:

"In my heart, Meesha, there are shadows
and images that sway, walk, and expand
like mist, but I am unable to give them
the form of words."[1]

In this letter Gibran not only reveals his true self; he gives a picture of his life, from which his doctrine on love stemmed. He does not seem to have had any real peace of mind. When love knocked at his door, he always experienced ecstasy, but this ecstasy was always marred to a certain extent by constant pain and sorrow, coming from various sources. It is easy to understand why Gibran keeps associating love with sorrow. He talks of "the pain of too much tenderness,"[2] the desires of the heart of the lover "to melt and be like a running brook that sings its melody to the night,"[3] to be wounded by your understanding of love and to bleed willingly and joyfully."[4]

Gibran seems to imply that pain is necessary for love. "This pain that accompanies love, invention and responsibility, also gives delight."[5] He finds also that what breaks the heart sings.[6]

When he first visited Selma Karamy, his sweetheart, he

felt this mixture of sweetness and bitterness which passionate lovers experience:

> I continued to meet Selma in that beautiful
> garden, gazing upon her beauty, marveling
> at her intelligence, and hearing the still-
> ness of sorrow. I felt an invisible hand
> drawing me to her.[7]

When Gibran was courting Selma with the almost sure prospect of not being able to marry her, he asked himself whether "her brightness, sweetness and grace opened my eyes and showed me the happiness and sorrow of love."[8] It is true that this double state of bliss and sorrow springs from the conflict that often "mars" a lover, as he puts it, when his visit with his beloved Selma was brought to an abrupt end with the announcement by Farris Effandi Karameh, her father, for her arranged marriage to the bishop's nephew:

> Those words uttered by Farris Effandi
> Karamy placed me side by side with his
> daughter at the altar of love. These
> words were a heavenly song which started
> with exaltation and ended with sorrow;
> they raised our spirits to the realm of
> light and searing flame; they were the
> cup from which we drank happiness and
> bitterness."[9]

THE RAGING TEMPEST

The two lovers, Gibran and Selma, found themselves in a situation where their love was frustrated by marriage brokers, and their sacred union violated by man-made laws and traditions. At that sad moment of love and sorrow, Gibran felt that sorrow linked their spirits and "each one saw in the other's face what the heart was feeling and heard the echo of a hidden voice." Their bodies were united by God and "their separation is nothing but agony."[10] However, this unity has a consoling effect on both lovers; "the sorrowful spirit finds rest when united with a similar one."[11] He compares their unity to a stranger who feels a little happy when he meets another stranger in a strange land. The strength of this union and understanding is beyond limit. Nothing can break it, not even the glory of happiness. He puts it in a very concrete way when he says:

> Hearts that are united through the medium
> of sorrow will not be separated by the
> glory of happiness. Love that is cleansed
> by tears will remain eternally pure and
> beautiful.[12]

While Gibran was sitting beside his beloved, enjoying food and sipping old wine, he confesses that "our souls were living in a world far away; we were dreaming of the future and its hardships."[13] Does this mean that for Gibran love is constantly marred by adversity and hardship? In this instance, no, as he was referring to the artificial interference of people, parents, traditions and man-made laws. But the writer can find no instance in which Gibran talks of love without lamenting the sorrow and bitterness that are mingled with it. This seems to stem from his Oriental background; most love songs of the East contain a constant complaint of a lover for not being loved enough, for not receiving enough attention and affection. The same refrain comes again and again but with a kind of conviction that love has its lights and its own force, which are immaterial and beyond the elements of this world. "If darkness hides the trees and flowers from our eyes, it will not hide love from our hearts."[14]

What happens to two lovers who experience both their love and its sorrow? Gibran confesses that when he attempted to console Selma by taking her hand and kissing it, "it was I who needed consolation more than she did."[15] What then did Gibran say? He resorted to his famous theory that "silence is the only eloquent language of strong love. I kept silent, thinking of our plight and listening to my heart beats; neither of us said more."[16]

Is there a contradiction in this theory of love and sorrow? Certainly. And Gibran makes Selma his mouthpiece to complain to the Lord for being in such a state of confusion and contradiction. She accuses the Lord of having opened her eyes to love, which then blinded her; of having kissed her with His lips and struck her with His strong hand; of having planted in her heart a white rose, but around the rose a barrier of thorns."[17]

Gibran's suffering at seeing his beloved suffer makes him also complain to the Almighty but in a more resigned and humble way; "Why hast Thou crushed me with Thy foot? Thou art a raging tempest, and I am like dust."[18] Hinting at Selma's marriage to another person than himself, he says "You will enter the gate of life, while I shall enter the gate of death . . . But I shall erect a statue of love and worship it in the valley of death."[19] Gibran remains logical with himself when he talks of love in some of his other writings, such as in *Sand and Foam*. He writes that you are a slave to him whom you love because you love him; and a slave to him who loves you because he loves you."[20] This aspect of love will remain a mystery. It is "a veil between lover and lover."[21] Difficulties and hardships in love seem to be chosen willingly by people, and this is due to a conflict between the mind and the heart. The latter is compared to a stream, the former to a sponge. Gibran confesses that it is not strange that most of us choose to absorb rather than run.[22]

CHAPTER VII

WEALTH — SYMBOL OF A DESPAIRING PEOPLE

Gibran's theory of love does not concede that wealth is a factor in uniting two hearts. He shows it in the story of *The Bridal Couch* when the bride shouts at the man whom she was forced to marry on account of his wealth:

"And you foolish man, who used wiles and
riches and treachery to make me a wife,
you are a symbol of a despairing people
seeking light in darkness and awaiting
the coming of water from out of a rock
and looking for the rose out of stony
ground . . . I forgive you in your small-
ness, for the spirit rejoicing in its
departure from the world pardons the sins
of the world."[1]

In another passage, he lets the woman who has deserted her husband and followed her beloved consider herself filthy and unclean before God, because she accepted his property that he might use her body. She became faithful and good when she ceased to trade her body for bread and her days for clothes.[2] This shows clearly that Gibran does not only favor divorce but also makes it a duty on woman to be "honest before God and the public." In *Sand and Foam* he writes, "how blind is he who gives you from his pocket that he may take from your heart."[3]

In *The Broken Wings* his beloved Selma says that her

father's wealth has placed her in the slave market. The man she married bought her though she neither knew nor loved him.⁴ Then Selma tells Gibran that he can think, talk, and act freely; he can write his name on the face of life because he is a man; he can live like a master because "your father's wealth will not place you in the slave market to be bought and sold; you can marry the woman of your choice and, before she lives in your home, you can let her reside in your heart and can exchange confidences without hindrance."⁵ We see clearly here that Gibran deplores and attacks the customs of the East which permit men to buy and sell a woman as a commodity. "The woman is looked upon as a commodity, purchased and delivered from one house to another."⁶⁵ But Gibran warns his generation that this state will not continue indefinitely because the woman is now aware of her situation, "in the past she walked blindly in the light, but now she walks open-eyed in the dark."

Gibran was painfully aware of the slavery of woman in the East and he waged a merciless campaign for her emancipation. The beauty of a woman was weighed in the balance with money without the necessary reciprocity of love that should exist between two hearts who wish to marry. In some instances, money was the sole aim of a marriage, without regard to the absence of mutual affection and love on the part of the partners. Gibran found that this was a catastrophe for society and in his works he gives many instances of miserable and unhappy women who were sold into marriage by marriage brokers interested in only fame and wealth.

Chapter VIII

TRADITION AND LAW —
LOVE MAKES THE LAW

In his basic doctrine on love Gibran rejects outright the intervention of any law in marriage and love. His concept of love is "divine," received at "God's command" and not made by man. For Gibran, this "divine and sacred love" is beyond man-made laws whether on the part of the church, parents or the public.

Gibran's meeting with Selma made him say that after the first hour with her ended "the will of Heaven freed me from the bondage of youth and solitude and let me walk in the procession of love";[1] in other words, Gibran feels that a divine love has freed him and now he is following the road of love imposed on him by God. Gibran also says in *Spirits Rebellious* that for the first time in his life he saw "the image of happiness standing between a man and a woman . . . whom dogma had condemned and law rejected."[2] This state of conflict is a problem to people, and Gibran recognized it. He believes that "love is what God reveals to the heart, while honor depends on the traditions of man."[3] For him "love is superior to law and traditions"; it is love which makes law. He illustrates this well when Wardeh El Hani justifies her divorce by saying that she had not known how to free herself until she "heard love summoning and saw the spirit girded for departure." Then she added that she knew that she had done nothing wrong, and she claimed that this order was given to her from Heaven, adding that "Heaven did not want me to spend my days crying out in agony, nor being unhappy and wretched, because in a man's happiness God is glorified."[4] Thus Gibran bases all his reasoning on the sacredness of love which is meant for man's happiness, since "by being happy man glorifies God." He also connects love with freedom as being the only freedom in the world because it so elevates the spirit that the laws of humanity and the phenomena of nature do not alter its course.[5]

CHAPTER IX

PARENTS AND FAMILY —
BOWS AND ARROWS

Gibran considers the mother as the essential person of the home and the one who most influences the children. In his *Spiritual Sayings* he writes: "Show me your mother's face: I will tell you who you are."[1] He keeps repeating that everything comes from the mother: character, intelligence, the manner of speaking and gesturing and even beauty.[2] He seems to relish in the idea that "children are the mirror of the mother."

Gibran cannot but return to the days of his childhood, saying that the most beautiful word on the lips of mankind is 'mother.'[3] Why is this so? The word 'mother' for him comes from the depth of the heart, therefore, it is sweet and kind. Also, mother is everything; "our consolation in sorrow, our hope in misery and our strength in weakness. She is the source of love, mercy, sympathy and forgiveness." Gibran finishes this description of mother by saying that he who loses his mother loses one who blesses and guards him constantly, who is the prototype of all existence and the eternal spirit, full of beauty and love.[4]

The word 'mother' is hidden in our hearts and it becomes to our lips in moments of both sorrow and happiness just as the perfume rises from the heart of the rose and mingles with clear and cloudy air.[5] "Even the germ of the race is in the mother's longing." Does he conclude that the mother's wishes can influence the yet unborn child? Maybe this superstition still prevailed in Gibran's time.

Everything in nature speaks of mother to Gibran. He compares her to the sun which is the mother of the earth by giving it its nourishment and its heat. This mother of the trees and the flowers, it produces, nurses and weans them. Finally he draws a comparison and extends it to the mother of all existence which is the eternal spirit, full of beauty and love.[6] When Selma died with her infant, Gibran commented that the child's grave was his mother's calm breast.[7]

The joy of a mother at holding her first baby is indescribable, especially when she can say for the first time: "My son." The love that exists between a mother and her child is something beyond belief. Nothing in the world can make a woman happier than becoming a mother.[8] He staunchly believes that the children often are the fruit of love and compassion.[9] He even makes a bold statement about the mother's love for her child regardless of his qualities and defects, when he asks whether the love of Judas' mother for her son was less than the love of Mary for Jesus?[10] In his *Spiritual Sayings* he draws a parallel similar to the idea of "the children are the mirror of the mother" and applies something similar to the father by saying that also the children are the mirror of the father: "I know his father; how do you expect me not to know him?" Which implies the sharing of many things between parents and children.

In *The Prophet* he says "your children are not your children. They are the sons and daughters of Life's longing for itself." By "Life's longing" Gibran probably means this natural tendency of man to perpetuate himself which could remind us of something similar to Schopenhauer's *will-to-live* and Bergson's *élan vital*. This terminology reflects somewhat the idea of Gibran's "Life's longing." Gibran continues by saying that "they come through you but not from you." He means that the child is from God and that parents are only instruments. He emphasizes clearly this divine intervention through them. "You may give them your love, but not your thoughts"; in other words, they are independent persons with their own ending life set by Divine Providence.

At the end Gibran indulges in paradox: "You may strive to be like them, but seek not to make them like you." He might mean that young children are not yet corrupted by man's vices, and the parents should try to be pure like them rather than to allow the children become like them. He compares God to the archer, the parents to the bows, and the children to the arrows when he says:

> You are the bows from which your children
> as living arrows are sent forth. The
> archer sees the mark upon the path of the
> infinite, and He bends you with His might.
> His arrows may go swift and far . . . For even
> as He loves the arrow that flies, so He
> loves also the bow that is stable.[11]

This shows the parents' relation in love and suffering with their children under the hand of the Almighty.

Chapter X

PEOPLE — "YES,
I LOVED YOU ALL"

The love of friends is deeply rooted in Gibran's doctrine of love. At first glance this love seems to be self-interested as when he says "Your friend is your needs answered."[1] But he continues: "He is your field which you sow with love and reap with thanksgiving. He is your board and your fireside." Our friend is the person to whom we come with our hunger and from whom we seek for peace. . . . We should not fear the "nay" when he speaks his mind nor should we withhold the "aye". When he is silent our heart should not cease to listen to his heart. In friendship, Gibran continues, all thoughts, all desires, all expectations are born and shared with joy. When we have a friend, we grieve because what we loved most in him becomes clearer and more tangible to us when the person loved is absent. The purpose of friendship should be "that of deepening the spirit." For if love seeks only the disclosure of its own mystery, it is not true love. If we receive from friendship, Gibran urges us to give what is best to our friend: if he must know the ebb of our tide, we should also let him know its flood. "The friend is to fill our need, but not our emptiness." In the sweetness of friendship are found laughter and a sharing of pleasure. The heart according to him finds its morning and its refreshment in little things like the dew.[2]

In *The Broken Wings* he recommends that a boy have

friends or companions in his games, otherwise his life will be like a narrow prison in which he sees nothing but spiderwebs and hears nothing but the crawling of insects.[3]

In *Sand and Foam* Gibran calls friendship "a sweet responsibility and never an opportunity." He creates in his writings the idea of a kind of universal family where "your most radiant garment is of the other person's table; your most comfortable bed is in the other person's house. He finally questions whether we can separate ourselves from others. Gibran shows that he understands how interpersonal relationship creates friendship and love among people when he said: "If it were not for guests all houses would be graves."

Although he finds that friendship and relationship with others are not without difficulties, he makes a difference between the person and his shortcomings when he says that he hates evil and sin while he loves the evildoer as well as the sinner; he hates diseases but he loves the person who is sick. So we see clearly that Gibran's philosophy towards others is completely opposed to the atheistic Sartrian conclusion that "Hell is other people."[4] Instead he adopts the Christian position that a person in society should share his life with others despite their faults, mistakes and shortcomings. He clearly stresses the importance of understanding and interpersonal relationship as the basis of this love. Such principles are also shared by Gabriel Marcel in *The Mystery of Being* when he emphasizes the need of understanding oneself through understanding others, which will bring a higher assertion of one's ego.[5]

Gibran obviously holds that if you expect a reward from loving your neighbor you are no longer in the domain of the virtue of love.[6] He also states that the love of neighbor must have a supernatural basis which requires sacrifice and understanding; "If you do not understand our friend under all conditions you will never understand him."[7] When Almustafa, Gibran's mouthpiece in *The Prophet* was on the point of leaving Orphalese he said:

In the stillness of the night I have
walked in your streets, and my spirit has
entered your houses, and your heart-beats
were in my heart and your breath was upon
my face, and I knew you all. It is in the
vast man that you are vast, and in behold-
ing him that I beheld you and loved you.
For what distances can love reach that are
not in that vast sphere? What visions,
what expectations and what presumptions
can outsoar that flight? Like a giant oak
tree covered with apple blossoms is the
vast man in you.[8]

From this quotation we learn Gibran's wide vision of
the love of other people. A neighbor who is not befriended
is indeed farther from us than the seven seas.[9] He cannot
limit it to a few but it must be given to all without discrim-
ination whatever. This is shown better in *The Forerunner*
in a poem entitled "love." He talks about the coexistence
of foes in the comparisons he makes when he says that
the "jackal and the mole drink from the same stream from
which the lion drinks" showing thus the need for co-existence.
Then he talks of love saying that it "has bridled my desires,
and raised my hunger and my thirst to dignity and pride,"
asking it under the form of prayer, "Let not the strong in
me and the constant eat the bread or drink the wine that
tempt my weaker self." He goes further to say that he
would prefer starving than take something which is not
for him. He also asks the Lord to let him become the prey
of the lion before the rabbit could become his (Gibran's)
own prey. This obviously shows that Gibran does not
want to be the instrument of overpowering the weak and
exploit and persecute him.

But this love of the weak does not mean that he does
not notice their need for improvement of their pitiful state.

"And you, the weak I have loved, though you have drained my faith and wasted my patience."[10]

His love for others was general: "I love the one among you as though he were all, and all as if you were one." He names the "giant and the pigmy, the leper and the anointed" and he goes so far as to say that he "loved the strong, though the marks of your iron hoofs are still upon my flesh." He does not forget the rich for whom he professes love "though bitter was your honey to my mouth." To the poor he expresses his love and feels ashamed of not being able to help them "though you knew my empty-handed shame." He loved also the poet "in-self-indulgence," whom he describes as having "borrowed lute and blind fingers," and the scholar "ever gathering rotted shrouds in potters' fields." Gibran continues his semi-sarcastic way of showing his love mingled with criticism. The priest, whom he loved also, he reproaches for sitting "in the silences of yesterday questioning the fate of tomorrow" and worshipping the "gods of the image of your own desires." He also expresses his love for the talkative who says that "life hath much to say" and for the dumb who says in silence that "which I fain would hear in words!" He loved also the judge and the critic despite their saying of him when he was "crucified": "He bleeds rhythmically, and the pattern his blood makes upon his white skin is beautiful to behold."[11]

In short, he loved all, "the young and the old, the trembling reed and the oak," but he complained also that this "overabundance of my heart turned you from me." Here he seems to imply that his love for them is positive, though he denounces their shortcomings:

> You would drink love from a cup, but
> not from a surging river. You would
> hear love's faint murmur, but when love
> shouts you would muffle your ears.[12]

Gibran hits back at those who want to discriminate in

his love, and who call him mockingly "the ageless one, the man without seasons . . . who assumes wisdom and understanding." They accuse him of being "too soft and yielding is his heart, and too undiscriminating is his path." Gibran rejects their idea that his love is that of a "weakling" and that "the strong loves only the strong."

> And because I have loved you overmuch
> you have said, 'It is but the love of a
> blind man who knows not the beauty of
> one and the ugliness of another. And it
> is the love of the tasteless who drinks
> vinegar even as wine. And it is the love
> of the impertinent and the overweening,
> for what stranger could be our mother and
> father and sister and brother?[13]

The only revenge he will take is that "I will love them more. Aye, even more. I will hide my love while seeming to hate, and disguise my tenderness as bitterness." Gibran then goes on to say that he "will wear an iron mask, and only when armed and mailed shall seek them." He then showers them with denunciations and ends his tirade:

> Thus with my lips have I denounced you,
> while my heart, bleeding within me, called
> you tender names. It was love lashed by
> its own self that spoke. It was pride
> half-slain that fluttered in the dust. It
> was my hunger for your love that raged from
> the housetop while my own love, kneeling in
> silence, prayed your forgiveness.[14]

Then he makes an unexpected statement: "It was my disguise that opened your eyes, and my seeming to hate that woke your hearts. And now you love me. You love the swords that strike you and the arrows that crave your breast." He ends his famous essay *The Last Watch* by saying that the Forerunner, his mouthpiece in the essay, "wept bitterly, for he knew in his heart that love humiliated in its nakedness is greater than love that seeks triumph in disguise; and he was ashamed." This beautiful essay is a masterpiece of the expression of Christian love based on understanding and the duty of fraternal correction while making distinction between the person and his shortcomings.

CHAPTER XI

SUMMARY AND CONCLUSIONS

Summary. Gibran's outlook on love has many sides and cannot be easily summarized without emasculating his thought and doing him injustice. Although he himself recognizes that he was a complicated personality, "I myself am a problem," we cannot deny that he breaks fresh ground in discussing love and its problems.

His main ideas center on the mystery of love. He confesses that after love invaded his heart he could no longer explain what it was, "when I knew love, the songs in my heart became a deep silence." He also says that love and suffering are inseparable. "It is a secret hand rough and sweet which takes hold of you in your loneliness and pours into your heart a drink in which bitterness and sweetness mingle." This mysterious love, which he calls "spiritual affinity," is "created in a moment." It is a call that comes from above without our consent. It is sent "at God's command" and "it directs our course."

"Sacred" and "divine" very often flow from his pen when he writes of love. "When you love you should not say 'God is in my heart'; but rather 'I am in the heart of God'." "Sacred" is often associated with "strength and depth" that are beyond human power. They make love "self-consuming and self-nourishing." According to him warm hearts do not need a source of heat outside themselves.

The happiness that love brings is necessarily connected with pain and even cruelty. He urges people "to be hurt, wounded and punished by your own understanding of love and then bleed willingly and joyfully." He compares this to "death that changes everything without itself being changed."

For Gibran beauty is a necessary element of love. But he does not consider that physical symmetry is essential. Beauty depends on "a spiritual accord between a man and a woman." Beauty is affected by our interior dispositions. He compares beauty to a "truth both open and secret, which we can understand only by love and touch only by virtue." For him "silence, love, beauty and virtue dwell together." He perceives that love does not need to speak much. Very often when love is at its height, silence is the only means of communication. The eyes, on the other hand, are the windows of the soul, and by their gaze lovers can communicate the depth and strength of their mutual emotions, be they bitter or sweet.

He holds that association with women is essential to man's development, "I am indebted for all that I call 'I' to women, ever since I was an infant." Later in his life he met women who remained a consolation to his intellectual as well as his emotional life. For him "every man loves two women; one is the creation of his imagination, and the other is not born." In other instances he writes of being "between two women who are for him like two lamps." He reproaches writers who complain that they cannot understand women, tracing their difficulty to their "looking at them through the veil of sex, and finding nothing except weakness and submission."

Marriage is based on the idea that love is given directly by God and therefore "sacred and divine." Love should not be contravened by social or church laws. He advocates that a woman who finds herself prey to marriage brokers should break with tradition and custom, and follow the "sacred inspiration of love." A woman should marry the man she really loves. He gives numerous instances of women being married to men on account of custom, wealth and tradition. They were unfortunates who led wretched lives. He defends the "unfaithful" woman who leaves such a husband, insisting that God does not want man to be miserable. In some of his writings we find that he hints at the "mistress type" of union, thus bypassing legal procedures and accepted ethics.

Conclusion. Gibran was excommunicated from the Maronite Catholic Church for his "poisonous and dangerous" writings in which he indiscriminately attacked the Church laws and her ministry. In his later works he also denied the divinity of Christ. Therefore, the Church sanction taken against him seems fully justified, despite the fact that Gibran was much concerned with the social problems plaguing his countrymen of that time. On the other hand, we would be quite narrow-minded to belittle the important insights which are found throughout his writings. For an intelligent reader, aware of these shortcomings, Gibran's writings can be quite beneficial and at times exciting.

A critic has to take into account all the aspects of the work of an author. Frankly speaking, if Gibran were writing today he would certainly meet a less hostile attitude since the Church now gives the faithful more latitude in the reading of the works by modern writers. This freedom requires maturity and a critical mind. Our generation seems to have this maturity and so deserves our trust in their ability to discriminate between what is orthodox and what is unacceptable.

It is common knowledge that the Church nowadays is becoming more understanding of human life and is making allowance for the possibility that lack of freedom in the choice of partners may render marriage null. This approximates to a certain extent the idea of Gibran that marriage should be contracted freely and out of love, and not because of tradition, custom and wealth. If it is proven that any of these factors has impaired free choice, the annulment of marriage will be decreed. We have to bear in mind that the rigid and defensive attitude that the Church had on marriage up till recently, comes from the Manichaeistic influence which considered sex pleasure as somehow sinful. Although the Church had condemned this erroneous doctrine, its influence has plagued Christian writers for many centuries, and we cannot expect that this rigidity and exaggerated fear of sex will disappear overnight.

On the whole we may safely say that for an intelligent reader, the works of Gibran can be helpful and even exciting, particularly in the sphere of love in general with its mixture of misunderstanding, sorrow and pain, as well as in its depth and strength which should be at the base of every true marriage.

BIBLIOGRAPHY

BIBLIOGRAPHY

A. PRIMARY SOURCES

Gibran, Kahlil. *The Broken Wings*. London: Heinemann, 1964. 82 pp.
——. *The Earth Gods*. London: Heinemann, 1962. 41 pp.
——. *The Forerunner*. London: Heinemann, 1963. 64 pp.
——. *The Garden of the Prophet*. London: Heinemann, 52 pp.
——. *Jesus, The Son of Man*. London: Heinemann, 187 pp.
——. *The Madman*. London: Heinemann, 1965. 73 pp.
——. *Nymphs of the Valley*. London: Heinemann, 1961. 55 pp.
——. *The Procession*. New York: The Philosophical Library, Inc., 1958. 74 pp.
——. *The Prophet*. London: Heinemann, 1967.
——. *Self-Portrait*. London: Heinemann, 1960. 94 pp.
——. *Spiritual Sayings*. London: Heinemann, 1966. 94 pp.
——. *Spirits Rebellious*. London: Heinemann, 1964.
——. *Thoughts and Meditations*. London: Heinemann, 117 pp.
——. *The Wanderer*. London: Heinemann, 1966, 92 pp.
Jaber, Jamil. *Joubran, Siratuhu, Adabuhu, Falsafatuhu wa Rasmuhu*. Beirut: Dar el Rihani, 1958. 224 pp.
Young, Barbara. *This Man from Lebanon*. New York: Alfred A. Knopf, 1945. 190 pp.

B. SECONDARY SOURCES

Atiyah, Edward. *The Arabs*. Great Britain: Penguin Books Inc., Harmondsworth, Middlesex, 1958. 250 pp.
Barrat, Denise. *Liban, scale du temps*. Paris: Editions du Centurion, 1967. 256 pp.
Cuming, Robert Denoon. *The Philosophy of Jean-Paul Sartre*. New York: The Modern Library, 1966. 185 pp.
Froom, Erich. *The Art of Loving*. London: Unwin Books, 1968. 96 pp.
Gilson, Etienne, Thomas Langan, and Arman A. Maurer, C. S. B., *A History of Philosophy*, Recent Philosophy. New York: Random House, 1966, 876 pp.
al Houeyyek, Youssef. *Zoukriati ma' Joubran*. Written by Edvique Juraydini Shaybub. Beirut: Dar el Ahad. 224 pp.
Jaber, Jamil. *May wa Joubran*. Beirut: Dar el Jamal, 1950. 80 pp.

The Jerusalem Bible. London: Carton, Longman & Todd, 1966. 500 pp.

Kirk, George E. *Contemporary Arab Politics.* New York: Frederick A. Praeger, 1961. 231 pp.

Lawrence, T. E. *Seven Pillars of Wisdom.* New York: Doubleday, Doran & Company, Inc., Garden City, 1935. 670 pp.

Lewis, Bernard. *The Arabs in History.* London: Arrow Books Hutchinson Ltd., 1958. 178 pp.

Lowell, Thomas. *With Lawrence in Arabia.* New York: Garden City, 1924. 408 pp.

Lindesmith, Alfred R. and Anselm L. Strauss. *Social Psychology.* New York: Holt, Rinehart and Winston, 1968. 450 pp.

Marcel, Gabriel. *The Mystery of Being.* (Chicago: Henry Regnery Company, 1960), pp. 8, 16.

Massoud, Habib. *Joubran, Hayyan wa Mayyitan.* Beirut: Dar el Riahni, 1966. 848 pp.

Naimeh, Mikhael. *Kahlil Gibran, His Life and His Work.* Beirut: Khayats, 1965. 280 pp.

————. *Al Majmou'at al Kamilat Li Mouallafat Joubran Kahlil Joubran.* Beirut: Dar Sader and Dar Beirut, 1959. 610 pp.

Saiegh, Tawfic. *Adhwa' Jadidah Ala Joubran.* Beirut: Dar al Sharquiah, 1966. 236 pp.

Tutsch, Hans E. *Facets of Arab Nationalism.* Canada: Ambassador Books, Ltd., Wayne State University Press, Detroit, 1965. 158 pp.

C. ENCYCLOPEDIA ARTICLES

Philip K. Hitti, "Arabic Language," *Encyclopedia Americana* (New York: International Headquarters: 575 Lexington Avenue, 1962), II, 123-124.

"Arabic Language," *Encyclopedia Britannica,* II, 185-186.

"Trojan War," *Encyclopedia Americana,* 27, p. 83.

"Cleopatra," *Encyclopedia Britannica,* 5, p. 80.

D. PERIODICALS AND NEWSPAPERS

Antoine Karam, "Joubran Al Khaled," *Les Conferences du Cenacle,* Xe annee (No. 5 - 1 Mai, 1956), pp. 245-247.

The National Catholic Reporter, July 21. 1-68.

Al Nahar (Beirut Arabic Daily), March 28, 1968.

FOOTNOTES

FOOTNOTES

CHAPTER I

1. *Huntchinson's New 20th Century Encyclopedia*, (Edited by E. M. Horsley, 1964), p. 823.
2. Edward Atiyah, *The Arabs* (Great Britain: Penguin Books Ltd., Harmondsworth, Middlesex, 1958), p. 19.
3. *Ibid.*, p. 49.
4. Edward Atiyah, *The Arabs* (*Great Britain,* Pelican Books, 1958), pp. 54-59.
5. Ibn Rushd, known in medieval Europe by the corrupted Latinized version of his name, Averroes, was the greatest of the Arab Aristotelian commentators — as he was indeed, whether in philosophy, jurisprudence, medicine or mathematics, one of the foremost figures of Arab civilization . . . Avecenna, or Ibn Sina, was the most influential of Arab civilization in the East . . . he was an encyclopedic figure, taking — in the phrase of Francis Bacon 'all knowledge for his province.' In Spain, there is one of almost equal stature — that of the philosopher Ibn Bajja (Avempace in the Latin version) who was a free-thinker and denied personal immortality. In the eastern Arab world, there lived about the same time al Ghazali, the greatest mystic thinker of Islam and a philosopher-theologian whose commentaries on Aristotle were . . . translated into Latin and exercised much influence over European thought.
6. Bernard Lewis, *The Arabs in History*, (London: Arrow Books, Hutchinson Ltd., 1958), p. 160.
7. *Op. Cit.*, p. 174.
8. *Ibid.*, p. 177.
9. The French name *Liban* comes from Latin: Libanus; the Arabic name: Loubnan, has kept the Semitic structure of the name: Lebnan . . . means: white, allusion to the constant snow which remains on the summit of the mountains for a good part of the year. (Jawad Boulos, *Les peuples et les civilisations du Proche-Orient*, tome I, p. 69, quoted by Denise Barrat, *Liban, escale du temps,* Paris, 1967. Editions du Centurion), p. 24.
10. Denise Barrat, *Liban, escale du temps*, (Paris: Editions du Centurion, 1967), p. 85.
11. *Ibid.*, p. 80.
12. *Op. Cit.*, pp. 46-48.
13. *Ibid.*, p. 49.

The 1966 statistics show that the number of Lebanese emigrants is almost equal to the present population of Lebanon.

Emigrants throughout the world are as follows: 400,000 in the United States; 350,000 in Brazil; 200,000 in Argentina; 40,000 in Mexico; 20,000 in Canada; 10,000 in Bolivia; 15,000 in Uruguay; 20,000 in Cuba; 10,000 in Equador; 10,000 in Chile; 20,000 in Central America; 25,000 in Australia; 2,000 in New Zealand; 70,000 in Africa; etc. . . . (Denise Barrat, p. 49.)

14. Barbara Young, *This Man from Lebanon* (New York: Alfred A. Knopf, 1945), Op. 36.

15. *Ibid.*, pp. 35-36.

16. Quoted by Alfred R. Lindesmith and Anselm L. Strauss, *Social Psychology.* (New York: Holt, Rinehart and Winston, 1968), p. 28.

17. *Encyclopedia Britannica*, Vol. II, p. 186. It gives the figure of fifty-million people speaking Arabic.

18. *Encyclopedia Britannica*, Vol. II, p. 196.

19. Young, *Op. Cit.*, p. 143.

20. Jamil Jaber, *Joubran, Siratuhu, Adabuhu, Falsafatuhu wa Rasmuhu* (Beirut: Dar el Rihani, 1958), p. 14.

21. Barbara Young, *This Man from Lebanon* (New York: Alfred A. Knopf, 1945), p. 143.

° His teacher at school had suggested that he abbreviate his name from Gibran Khalil Gibran to Khalil Gibran, and by this name he became known to his American friends. (George Kheirallah in his biographical sketch added to *The Procession*, p. 13).

22. Jaber, *op. cit.*, p. 18.

23. *Ibid.*

24. Young, *op. cit.*, p. 9.

25. Barbara Young quoted by Jaber, *op. cit.*, p. 18.

26. Barbara Young, *op. cit.*, p. 9.

27. George Kheirallah, *op. cit.*, p. 16.

28. *Ibid.* p. 12.

29. Mikhael Naimeh, quoted by Jaber, *op. cit.*, p. 21.

30. Jaber, *op. cit.*, p. 21.

31. *Ibid.*, p. 24.

° Some of the classical writers of the *Aljahiliah* period or pre-Islamic era known as "period of ignorance" or *Al Ahd El Jahili*. These names are quite familiar to grade school students in the Arab World.

32. Young, *op. cit.*, p. 19.

33. Jaber, *op. cit.*, p. 32.

34. Kheirallah, *op. cit.*, p. 20.

35. Young, *op. cit.*, p. 57.

36. *Ibid.*

37. Mikhail Naimeh, *Al Majmou'at al Kamilat Li Mouallafat Joubran Khalil Joubran* (Beirut: Dar Sader and Dar Beirut, 1959), p. 29.

10. Kahlil Gibran, *Thoughts and Meditations* (London: Heinemann, 1966), p. 184.
11. *Ibid.*, p. 18.
12. Gibran, *The Broken Wings, op. cit.*, p. 41.
13. Kahlil Gibran, *Self Portrait* (London: Heinemann, 1960), p. 34.
14. Gibran, *The Broken Wings, op. cit.*, p. 13.
15. Kahlil Gibran, *Spirits Rebellious* (London: Heinemann, 1964), p. 10.
16. Gibran, *The Broken Wings, op. cit.*, p. 13.
17. *Ibid.*, p. 25.
18. *Ibid.*, p. 24.
19. *Ibid.*, p. 21.
20. *Ibid.*, p. 24.
21. Gibran, *Spirits Rebellious, op. cit.*, p. 52.
22. Gibran, *Sand and Foam* (London: Heinemann, 1968), p. 20.
23. Etienne Gilson, Thomas Langan, Armand A. Maurer, C. S. B., *A History of Philosophy* (New York: Random House, 1966), citing Henri Bergson, "The Stream of Consciousness".
24. Gibran, *Self Portrait, op. cit.*, p. 80.
25. Kahlil Gibran, *Spiritual Sayings* (London: Heinemann, 1966), p. 51.
26. Kahlil Gibran, *The Prophet* (London: Heinemann, 1964), p. 12.
28. *Ibid.*
29. Gibran, *Sand and Foam, loc. cit.*
30. Kahlil Gibran, *The Broken Wings* (London: Heinemann, 1957), p. 25.
31. *Ibid.*, p. 32.
32. Gibran, *Sand and Foam, op. cit.*, p. 21.
33. Gibran, *The Broken Wings, ibid.*, p. 41.
34. Gibran, *Spirits Bebellious, op. cit.*, p. 46.
35. *Ibid.*, p. 48.
36. *Ibid.*, p. 50.
37. *Ibid.*
38. *Ibid.*
39. Gibran, *Thoughts and Meditations, op. cit.*, p. 16.
40. Gibran, *The Prophet, op. cit.*, p. 8.
41. Gibran, *The Broken Wings, op. cit.*, p. 23.
42. *Ibid.*, p. 9.
43. *Ibid.*, p. 21.
44. *Ibid.*, p. 25.
45. *Ibid.*, p. 45.
46. *Ibid.*, p. 13.
47. Gibran, *Spirits Rebellious, op. cit.*, p. 82.
48. Gibran, *The Broken Wings, op. cit.*, p. 1.
49. Kahlil Gibran, *Self Portrait* (London: Heinemann, 1960), p. 62.
50. Gibran, *Spirits Rebellious, op. cit.*, p. 82.
51. Gibran, *The Broken Wings, op. cit.*, p. 19.

38. Massoud Habib, *Joubran, Hayyan wa Mayyitan* (Beirut: Dar el Riahni, 1966), p. 539.

39. *Ibid.*, p. 560.

40. *Ibid.*, p. 559.

41. Habib Massoud, *Joubran, Hayyan wa Mayyitan* (Beirut: Dar el Riahni, 1966), p. 20.

42. *Ibid.*, p. 21.

43. Barbara Young, *This Man from Lebanon* (New York: Alfred A. Knopf, 1945), p. 33.

44. Massoud, *op. cit.*, p. 21.

45. *Ibid.*

46. *Ibid.*

47. *Ibid.*

48. *Ibid.*, citing Barbara Young, *This Man From Lebanon* (New York: Alfred A. Knopf, 1945).

49. *The National Catholic Reporter,* July 21, 1968.

50. *Al Nahar,* March 28, 1968.

51. Jamil Jaber, *Joubran, Siratuhu, Arabuhu, Falsafatuhu wa Rasmuhu* (Beirut: Dar el Rihani, 1958), p. 47.

52. Kahlil Gibran, *The Broken Wings* (London: Heinemann, 1964), p. 8.

53. Jamil Jaber, *May wa Joubran* (Beirut: Dar el Jamal, 1950), p. 8.

54. *Ibid.*, p. 8.

55. Mikhael Naimeh, *Kahlil Gibran, His Life and His Work* (Beirut: Khayats, 1965), p. 155.

56. *Ibid.*, p. 24.

57. Antoine Karam, "Joubran al Khaled," *Les Conferences du Cenacle* (Xe année, No. 5 - 1 Mai, 1956), p. 245.

58. Jamil Jaber, *Joubran, Siratuhu, Adabuhu, Falsafatuhu wa Rasmuhu* (Beirut: Dar el Rihani, 1958), pp. 32-33.

CHAPTER II

1. Habib Massoud, *At The Gate of The Temple*, p. 53.

2. *Ibid.*

3. *Ibid.*

4. *Ibid.*, p. 54.

5. *Ibid.*

6. *Ibid.*, p. 55.

7. *Ibid.*

8. Erich Fromm, *The Art of Loving* (London: Unwin Books, 1968), p. 5.

9. Kahlil Gibran, *The Broken Wings* (London: Heinemann, 1957), p. 23.

52. *Ibid.*, p. 33.
53. *Ibid.*, p. 17.
54. *Ibid.*, p. 33.
55. *Ibid.*, p. 10.
56. Kahlil Gibran, *Spiritual Sayings* (London: Heinemann, 1966), p. 23.
57. *Ibid.*, p. 48.
58. Kahlil Gibran, *Sand and Foam* (London: Heinemann, 1957), p. 7.
59. Gibran, *The Broken Wings, op. cit.*, p. 11.
60. Gibran, *Spiritual Sayings, op. cit.*, p. 13.
61. Kahlil Gibran, *Self-Portrait* (London: Heinemann, 1960), p. 34.
62. Kahlil Gibran, *The Forerunner* (London: Heinemann, 1963), p. 60.
63. Kahlil Gibran, *The Forerunner* (London: Heinemann, 1963), p. 62.
64. *Ibid.*
65. *Ibid.*
66. *Ibid.*
67. Gibran, *Self Portrait* (London: Heinemann, 1960), p. 35.
68. Kahlil Gibran, *The Broken Wings* (London: Heinemann, 1957), p. 62.
69. *Ibid.*, p. 70.
70. *Ibid.*, p. 12.
71. Kahlil Gibran, *Sand and Foam* (London: Heinemann, 1968), p. 21.
72. *Ibid.*, p. 50.
73. *Ibid.*, p. 21.
74. Kahlil Gibran, *The Broken Wings* (London: Heinemann, 1957), p. 25.
75. *Ibid.*, p. 32.

CHAPTER III

1. Kahlil Gibran, *Self Portrait* (London: Heinemann, 1960), p. 20.
2. Kahlil Gibran, *Thoughts and Meditations* (London: Heinemann, 1966), p. 24.
3. Kahlil Gibran, *The Broken Wings* (London: Heinemann, 1957), p. 11.
4. *Ibid.*
5. *Ibid.*, p. 14.
6. *Ibid.*
7. *Ibid.*, p. 15.
8. *Ibid.*, p. 9.
9. *Ibid.*, p. 19.
10. Kahlil Gibran, *The Broken Wings* (London: Heinemann, 1957), p. 33.

CHAPTER IV

1. Kahlil Gibran, *Self Portrait* (London: Heinemann, 1960), p. 84.
2. Jamil Jaber, *Joubran, Siratuhu, Adabuhu, Falsafatuhu wa Rasmuhu* (Beirut: Dar el Rihani, 1958), p. 21.
3. *Ibid.*, p. 27.
4. Kahlil Gibran, *The Broken Wings* (London: Heinemann, 1964), p. 50.
5. Kahlil Gibran, *Sand and Foam* (London: Heinemann, 1968), p. 21.
6. Gibran, *Self Portrait, op. cit.*, p. 58.
7. Gibran, *The Broken Wings, op. cit.*, p. x.
8. Kahlil Gibran, *Spirits Rebellious* (London: Heinemann, 1964), p. 11.
9. Gibran, *Sand and Foam, op. cit.*, p. 14.
10. Kahlil Gibran, *The Forerunner* (London: Heinemann, 1963), p. 59.
11. Gibran, *The Broken Wings, op. cit.*, p. 9.
12. *Ibid.*
13. *Ibid.*
14. *Ibid.*, p. 63.
15. *Ibid.*, p. 21.
16. Kahlil Gibran, *Spiritual Sayings* (London: Heinemann, 1966), p. 19.
17. Gibran, *Sand and Foam, op. cit.*, p. 12.
18. Gibran, *The Broken Wings, op. cit.*, p. 34.
19. *Ibid.*
20. *Ibid.*
21. *Ibid.*, p. 23.
22. *Ibid.*, p. 25.
23. *Ibid.*, p. 64.
24. Gibran, *Spiritual Sayings, op. cit.*, p. 31.
25. *Ibid.*
26. Gibran, *Sand and Foam* (London: Heinemann, 1968), p. 21.
27. Gibran, *Spirits Rebellious, op. cit.*, p. 16.
28. *Ibid.*
29. Jaber, *Joubran, Siratuhu, Adabuhu, Falsafatuhu wa Rasmuhu, op. cit.*, p. 82.
30. *Ibid.*
31. Mikhael Naimeth, *Kahlil Gibran, His Life and His Work* (Beirut: Khayats, 1965), p. 79.
32. *Ibid.*, p. 89.
33. *Ibid.*, p. 90.
34. *Ibid.*, p. 89.

CHAPTER V

1. Kahlil Gibran, *Spiritual Sayings* (London: Heinemann, 1966), p. 14.
2. *Ibid.*, p. 13.
3. Kahlil Gibran, *The Prophet* (London: Heinemann, 1967), p. 16.
4. Kahlil Gibran, *Spirits Rebellious* (London: Heinemann, 1964), p. 10.
5. Gibran, *loc. cit.*
6. Gibran, *The Prophet, op. cit.,* p. 19.
7. Gibran, *Spirits Rebellious, op. cit.,* p. 9.
8. *Ibid.*, p. 10.
9. Gibran, *Spirits Rebellious, op. cit.,* p. 10.
10. *Ibid.*, p. 19.
11. *Ibid.*, p. 1.
12. *Ibid.*, p. 9.
13. Kahlil Gibran, *The Broken Wings* (London: Heinemann, 1964), p. 30.
14. Gibran, *Spirits Rebellious, op. cit.,* p. 31.
15. *Ibid.*
16. *Ibid.*, p. 13.

CHAPTER VI

1. Kahlil Gibran, *Self Portrait* (London: Heinemann, 1960), p. 67.
2. Kahlil Gibran, *The Prophet* (London: Heinemann, 1967), p. 12.
3. *Ibid.*
4. *Ibid.*
5. Kahlil Gibran, *Spiritual Sayings* (London: Heinemann, 1966), p. 22.
6. *Ibid.*
7. Kahlil Gibran, *The Broken Wings* (London: Heinemann, 1964), p. 13.
8. *Ibid.*, p. 12.
9. Gibran, *The Broken Wings, op. cit.,* p. 13.
10. *Ibid.*, p. 16.
11. *Ibid.*
12. *Ibid.*
13. *Ibid.*, p. 18.
14. *Ibid.*, p. 20.
15. *Ibid.*, p. 43.
16. *Ibid.*
17. *Ibid.*
18. *Ibid.*, p. 42.

19. *Ibid.*, p. 40.
20. Kahlil Gibran, *Sand and Foam* (London: Heinemann, 1968), p. 24.
21. *Ibid.*, p. 21.

CHAPTER VII

1. Kahlil Gibran, *Spirits Rebellious* (London: Heinemann, 1964), p. 52.
2. *Ibid.*, p. 13.
3. Kahlil Gibran, *Sand and Foam* (London: Heinemann, 1968), p. 32.
4. Kahlil Gibran, *The Broken Wings* (London: Heinemann, 1964), p. 36.
5. *Ibid.*
6. *Ibid.*

CHAPTER VIII

1. Kahlil Gibran, *The Broken Wings* (London: Heinemann, 1964), p. 12.
2. Kahlil Gibran, *Spirits Rebellious* (London: Heinemann, 1964), p. 12.
3. *Ibid.*, p. 47.
4. *Ibid.*, p. 19.
5. Gibran, *The Broken Wings, op. cit.*, p. 12.

CHAPTER IX

1. Kahlil Gibran, *Spiritual Sayings* (London: Heinemann, 1966), p. 62.
2. Kahlil Gibran, *The Broken Wings* (London: Heinemann, 1964), p. 53.
3. *Ibid.*, p. 54.
4. *Ibid.*
5. *Ibid.*, p. 55.
6. Kahlil Gibran, *Self Portrait* (London: Heinemann, 1960), p. 9.
7. Gibran, *The Broken Wings, op. cit.*, p. 81.

8. *Ibid.*, p. 77.
9. *Ibid.*
11. Kahlil Gibran, *The Prophet* (London: Heinemann, 1967), p. 20.

CHAPTER X

1. Kahlil Gibran, *The Prophet* (London: Heinemann, 1967), p. 69.
2. *Ibid.*, p. 69-70.
3. Kahlil Gibran, *The Broken Wings* (London: Heinemann, 1964), p. 3.
4. Robert Denoon Cumming, *The Philosophy of Jean-Paul Sartre* (New York: The Modern Library, 1966), p. 185.
5. Gabriel Marcel, *The Mystery of Being* (Chicago: Henry Regnery Company, 1960), pp. 8, 16.
6. Kahlil Gibran, *Sand and Foam* (London: Heinemann, 1968), p. 55.
7. *Ibid.*, p. 22.
8. Gibran, *The Prophet, op. cit.*, p. 101.
9. Kahlil Gibran, *The Garden of the Prophet* (London: Heinemann, 1964), p. 15.
10. Kahlil Gibran, *The Forerunner* (London: Heinemann, 1963), p. 58.
11. *Ibib.*, p. 57-64.
12. *Ibid.*, p. 60.
13. *Ibid.*, p. 58.
14. *Ibid.*, p. 62.

OTHER WORKS OF GIBRAN
IN THIS SERIES: